LB
1027
V64

Voight, Ralph Claude.
Invitation to learning; the learning center handbook, by Ralph Claude Voight, in consultation with Jean Butler ₁and others₁ Illus. by Paul Butler. Foreword by John Nickols. Washington, Acropolis Books ₁1971₁

149 p. illus. 26 cm. $4.95

1. Teaching—Aids and devices.　I. Title.　II. Title: Learning center handbook.

LB1027.V64　　　　　371.3′078　　　　79–150992

ISBN 0–87491–318–7 ·　　　　　**7 2**　　　　MARC

INVITATION TO LEARNING

THE LEARNING CENTER HANDBOOK

INVITATION TO LEARNING

THE LEARNING CENTER HANDBOOK

BY
RALPH CLAUDE VOIGHT

in consultation with
Jean Butler
A. B. Costea, Jr.
Raymond A. O'Neill
Carmen Wilkinson

illustrated by
Paul Butler

FOREWORD BY JOHN NICKOLS, PH.D.

Published by ACROPOLIS BOOKS LTD. • Washington, D. C. 20009

ACROPOLIS BOOKS
Colortone Building, 2400 17th St., N.W.
Washington, D.C. 20009

Printed in the United States of America by
COLORTONE PRESS, Creative Graphics Inc.
Washington, D.C. 20009

Library of Congress Catalog Number 79-150992

Standard Book No. 87491-318-7

ACKNOWLEDGMENTS

My concept of the Learning Center as a "teaching method" has developed at a gradual pace and specific educational experiences have influenced its development. I am especially indebted to:

1958-60   Dr. Francis Holiday who was teaching at American University and involved a college student into the then-unknown world of the Interest Corner and Station for individualizing instruction.

1962-64   Mrs. Weeta Morris, Principal at Edward U. Taylor elementary school in Montgomery County, Maryland, whose guidance and patience assisted a 5th grade teacher in implementing Interest Centers into the curriculum as a vehicle for organizing content for the individual.

1966-67   The teachers in Region II of West Virginia who developed social studies units with large group and individual task assignments designed to individuals instruction.

1967-69   Mrs. Kathern Crone, former principal of Germantown elementary school in Montgomery County, Md. who provided many interesting discussion periods on the topic ATLUOP.*

1969   The Arlington and Fairfax County, Virginia teachers of Education 120, University of Virginia, who along with the professor defined types and designs of Learning Centers for the 70's.

*ATLUOP is an Administrator-Teacher-Learner Unit Organizational Pattern for the total staff to use when planning open-ended learning activities for the individual student on a social studies theme that is being studied by all grades in the school, K-6.

Involve the child in learning

FOREWORD

For a new idea to be implemented successfully in modern day schools, it must meet three essential criteria: (1) It must be the outgrowth of face-to-face work with the students; (2) It must suit the needs of the students as individuals in their own right; (3) It must lend itself to gradual implementation, step by step as the user works at his own pace in developing the necessary know-how.

School officials might facilitate the implementation of a new idea in several ways. They might prepare the administration to understand and support the idea through the use of staff development programs which upgrade the process of obtaining and interpreting information from all phases of the field operations. They might expand inservice programs to provide appropriate exposure and guidance for initiating and developing the use of the new idea. They might facilitate the use of the new idea through opening communication channels for field personnel to report on successes, failures, and modifications in order to build a system for information exchange. They might encourage field personnel to develop ''teams'' of principals or specialists who work to perfect modifications which are suited to the conditions or problems a given number of schools seem to have in common with one another. They might broaden the use of consultants who are free to communicate and to work with the total range of personnel, from the students and the teachers to the superintendent and the school board.

One of the few ideas which might meet the three essential criteria for successful implementation under conditions which offer less than optimal facilitation are contained in Invitation to Learning by Ralph C. Voight. Mr. Voight offers a practical approach to education which might be implemented either by an individual teacher to serve individual children in a single classroom or by a group of teachers or specialists working along with one another.

Voight's Learning Center approach is anchored to the needs of the individual student, to the student's own desire for involvement and to the continually improving classroom atmosphere rather than to the manner in which the schools are administered. This approach, then, need not be avoided when optimal facilitation is not forthcoming.

The teacher might call upon his own desire, flexibility, and resourcefulness and begin implementation according to the teacher's own interests, skills, cooperative efforts, and freedom to operate. He might inform himself through the use of available literature, use this information and Mr. Voight's contributions to expand upon his own preparation, and proceed step by step to build a frame of reference for establishing his own learning center classroom. (Chances are that the program will sell itself and facilitation will emerge sometime in the future.)

The Learning Center approach truly meets the first criterion for successful implementation. Mr. Voight and his associates spent many years in classroom situations sorting relevant procedures and concepts from irrelevant ones until their experiences could be organized into printed form and shared with others. Invitation to Learning permits teachers to benefit from Mr. Voight's experiences and to start with a sense of guidance well along the way toward implementation, thereby permitting them to avoid a multitude of the frustrations which might have been encountered otherwise in the process of developing a new approach of their own. The descriptions of the different Learning Centers, alone, permit a degree of freedom to explore alternative instructional procedures which could emerge only from first-hand experience.

The text of the book itself shows that the idea of a Learning Center approach meets the second criterion for successful implementation, that it must allow for individual instruction. Perhaps the major reason for this is the flexibility which the different types of Learning Centers offer in planning individualized programs.

Consider three different categories for Learning Centers which can be established in a given classroom. These might be described as the Inventory, the Academic, and the Developmental Learning Centers.

The Inventory Learning Center (or LC) might be located at a table or at four to six carrel-like structures where each child is evaluated periodically through the use of teacher-made or standardized instruments. His status in reading, spelling, arithmetic, abstract thinking, problem-solving, etc., can be appraised for the purpose of planning appropriate preventive, catch-up, and improvement exercises in addition to a basic core of regular classroom activities. The patterns of strengths and weaknesses can be used to proportion classroom time according to need, interest, and achievement. A relevant objective is to identify where each child is functioning and to permit him to begin where he is and proceed at his own pace in a variety of functions.

The Academic LCs might be designed to permit each child to experience personal involvement in the usual school subjects. Some of these LCs might be large enough to accommodate regular work with groups. Others might be used to lend support, breadth, or depth to the usual classroom subjects. Still others might be designed around single concept topics.

Many Academic LCs, however, might incorporate the usual classroom subject matter, appropriately designed instructional procedures, and the specialized types of activities into a combined approach to learning, hopefully through the use of discovery as well as practice. Consider the Project LCs where teacher and child plan together in order to enrich experiences of the individual child through the commercially prepared sequence materials. Unit LCs might be designed around the use of central themes selected from the regular classroom curriculum on social studies, the use of specific axioms in math, etc. Student LCs might be designed to permit the student to generate his own topic of study.

One of the most innovative contributions to modern day education might well be contained in Mr. Voight's work. Specifically, his discussions of the Cooperative, the Fun, the Prescriptive, and the Skill Development LCs provide ample flexibility for designing Developmental LCs. A Developmental LC is defined as one which emphasizes process, rather than content. Its value is not derived from the subject matter itself, but, rather, from what the child does and from the functions which are exercised during the process of learning. Here, the child is permitted to cultivate basic processes regardless of the materials used or the knowledge to be gained. For example, two children might engage in a game of classification in order to gain experience in the process of classifying pictures, even when they fail to discover specified sub-groupings which were built into the pictures.

The Cooperative LC would be established to permit the student (or students) and teacher to plan specific activities together and to design the activities accordingly. If they agree that a certain type of information is to be acquired, it would be classified as an Academic LC. If they agree that certain learning functions are to be exercised, it would be classified as a Developmental LC and the activities would start at a relatively low level of difficulty and proceed upward.

A relevant objective would be to build upon consensual experience which helps to develop basic skills and knowledge useful in language retention and usage. Two students might sit across from one another and make, color, or label pieces for a doll house, helping one another in the process of calling upon their past experiences and expressing them verbally. Two children might exercise the expression of common experiences through pantomime. They could gain skill in learning from one another through the use of language experience and language arts activities. Games involving words and numbers could be appropriate.

A Fun LC permits tasks to be enjoyed without being justified. Apparent free-learning and social interaction can be encouraged. For example, this LC might consist of no more than a large, well-padded rug where two or more children can interact with one another in developmental games, socio-drama, motoric exercises, or discussion.

The Prescriptive LCs permit the teacher (or others) to design special activities to meet the needs of individual children. Such activities might involve discovery, strategy, problem-solving, or analytical thinking. Prescriptions can be as unique as the teacher, or teacher and child, can tailor them.

The Skill Development LCs are as timely as the movement to help children with learning disabilities. Psychomotor and perceptual exercises, e.g., those involving copying, concentration, listening, and observation, are specifically appropriate here.

The third criterion for successful implementation emphasizes the role of the teacher. Mr. Voight's work makes it possible to start with one activity and to modify it or to add new ones as more is learned about individual students. The Inventory LC can often be used to start a program, with other LCs being added as the inventory data and classroom observation reveal the needs of the individuals.

It is very difficult to imagine an approach which is as fertile and permits as much flexibility in preparing educators to promote total child development. The use of cognitive tests can be used along with teacher-made tests and classroom observation in a manner which permits either the teacher or the student to begin where he is and proceed at his own pace. The fact that regular curriculum and specialized developmental activities can be integrated into the total classroom program should make it possible for the concept of a Learning Center Classroom to become synonymous with concepts of the ungraded and the individualized classroom.

Invitation to Learning must be considered one of the most important educational products available today. It is a must for every educator and teacher. Even if the Learning Center approach is not to be adopted in a given school, the ideas to be derived from this book will be helpful in retooling one's thinking in the direction of meeting the individual needs of students with learning disabilities, average achievement, and advanced development.

—John Nickols, Ph.D.

To the Reader:

The single concept film loop or the mini-class suggests a delimited and selective idea. It is this concept that is projected in this "Survival Kit." One and only one preoccupation prompts this endeavor — it is the production of an operational tool (guide, manual, handbook) for teachers who want a practical aid to individualization of learning. Like any survival kit, brevity characterizes it. Essentials only. A compass, a basic first aid packet, and an inflatable life raft—functional and operational. Likewise this kit.

Section I sets the stage with a discussion of the idea of the Learning Center. Section II offers practical and realistic hints and tips relative to getting under way. Section III presents "child-tested" Learning Centers. Section IV reviews the most asked questions about Learning Centers.

INTRODUCTION

As children grow and change, so must the methods of classroom teaching evolve and change. The teaching practices used by teachers should be based on the best knowledge they have of child growth and development.

A foundation stone that has long been recognized but not fully implemented, is the concept of individual differences. Each child possesses personal, unique characteristics. Classroom practices must reflect this reality more consistently if they are to provide appropriate learning experiences for each child.

In the '70's, the major classroom tactic must be guided by child growth and development and child individuality. The establishment of the Learning Center is directed toward this end. The Learning Center classroom focuses the teacher's sights on each child—enhancing the opportunities for meeting the personal needs of the learner. The Learning Center, emerging as a definable teaching method, is providing teachers with a viable means to achieve this end.

—R. C. V.

TABLE OF CONTENTS

SECTION III—EXAMPLES

SECTION IV—QUESTIONS ABOUT CENTER INVENTION

Centers: Past

A review of much of the writing about Interest Centers in the '60's expresses such notions as—

- every classroom should have an Interest Center of some sort.

- a corner should be set aside, sometimes quite purposefully, sometimes quite casually.

- some Interest Centers may be places designed to stimulate interest, curiosity, critical thinking.

- Interest Centers may be a source of a *busy hum*, and not, therefore, undesirable.

- Interest Centers should not be substitutes for a curriculum.

Some Interest Centers even had titles and stated purposes, e.g.,

TITLE	PURPOSE
"Game and Toy Center"	Stimulate thinking
"Listening Center"	Other teacher
"Composing Center"	Inner thoughts
"Library Center"	Heart of classroom
"Art Center"	Creative expression
"Science Center"	Searching mind
"Play-acting"	Exchange position
"Holidays"	Culture

Concern was evidently moving toward a practical methodology through which to appeal to individuality in children. However, there were problems. In some Centers, the child saw no real point to the activity. A beginning and ending were only vaguely implied. Teachers found it difficult to justify extensive use of Centers. The Interest Centers could serve only limited demands of the classroom.

Even though most of the writing of the '60's probably suggests a preoccupation by teachers with many aspects of individual differences, ways to implement the idea remained remote for most teachers.

Centers: Future

The Learning Center, fully developed, implies certain characteristic behaviors on the part of the teacher, an enlarged learning environment, greater independence on the part of the learner, and revised physical arrangements in the classroom. The Learning Center of the future embodies the implementation of an idea—each child will grow at his own rate, in his own style, and to his uniquely personal potential. The Learning Center can provide a highly personal experience for the child, and can facilitate learning through a feedback system. The Learning Center within this pattern becomes a process offering an orderly, contextual experience.

Criteria for Establishing Centers

When a teacher or team of teachers or an entire school staff has elected to proceed toward the initiation of the personalized learning configuration of the Learning Center method, the following criteria should be kept in mind at all times:

> Each Learning Center should contribute to the achievement of the purposes of the individual. From Learning Center to Learning, the child should be confronted with opportunities to work with basic skills, facts, concepts, and large ideas.
>
> The Learning Center should deal with a significant area of study that is of interest to the student. It should be openended so that individual creativity can be fostered. It should

provide opportunities to develop problem solving, critical thinking, and creative thinking. It should provide opportunities that constantly lead the individual to strive to compete with himself toward higher levels of learning.

Learning experiences at the Center should be related to past personal experiences and should lead to broader and deeper new experiences.

Learning Center activities should have practical time limits related to the child's developmental level which will permit completion of the tasks.

Directions at each Learning Center should assist the student in gaining an overview of the task quickly. The directions need to be clearly stated so that the student understands where to begin and when he has completed the task successfully.

The design of Learning Centers depends on the types of experiences to be made available *to the student*.

The teacher electing to establish Learning Centers must provide a variety of faces for the Centers. Humor, sparkle, and intrigue injected into the Centers will pay high dividends. Use this checklist to appraise the diversity of your Centers. Learning Centers should:

- involve each child actively.

- confront the child with essential skill–developing activities.

- tempt the child to stretch his imagination and creativity in the pursuit of divergent reaction to problems that offer no pat solution.

- provoke the child's interest so that he finds himself engrossed in processes or systems of fundamental significance, such as, cause and effect, "such as, . . . then what?"

- immerse the child in conditions leading to the development of concepts or generalizations inferred from facts.

- tease the child's sense of humor.

- team the child with one or more classmates in a joint-action task where cooperation and interaction present opportunities for the development of human relations skills.

- offer free or controlled choices from among many challenging and intriguing locations about the classroom.

- intensify learning activities through the use of listening and recording devices, or with viewing and projection equipment, or both.

Organizing for Learning Centers

Through the Learning Center method of ordering a classroom, the teaching act may involve just one teacher or all the teachers on a staff. A teacher, in concert with the principal and/or a curriculum specialist, may elect to establish Learning Centers. He may wish to add a few Centers in a regular self-contained classroom choosing to emphasize material for Centers that support a basic skill program or which relate to a unit of study in Social Studies or Science, or merely add a complementary or enriching element to the classroom.

On the other hand, the teacher may elect to alter his course and convert his self-contained, somewhat traditional classroom and methodology to a total Learning Center scheme in which case the types and numbers of Centers are increased proportionately.

Another organizational configuration might involve a grouping of two or more teachers. A team or cooperative teaching arrangement between or among teachers might adopt total or partial Learning Center instruction. Finally, an entire building might decide to convert to a Learning Center method of teaching.

Since Learning Centers aim at individuality, a Center in the "second grade" ought to be useful to any other child if it fits his maturity, interests, and learning style without regard to grade level. Learning Centers can be a stepping stone to "ungrading" or "non-grading" a school. The process may begin at grades K-3, or it may go school-wide—but Learning Centers can help.

Physical Setting for Learning Centers

A very practical matter which must not be neglected is the actual physical arrangements for Centers in the classroom. The teacher must manage the room and its furnishings so as to produce a facilitating environment. These considerations range from the size and shape of the room to the kinds and numbers of tables, carrels, or easels used. Proper lighting must be available to each Center. Arrangements should be such that children can (and may) move freely from place to place with a minimum of disturbance to others. Chairs, work areas, and tools should be comfortable. Learning Centers themselves should be attractive.

It takes time and energy to get this extra touch but the children can be a great help to the teacher if he plans for it in advance.

To summarize, Learning Centers should be set up to provide interesting, attractive places to work and should allow a free traffic flow throughout the room. (See Section III, pages 35-42 for examples).

Goal Setting of Learning Centers

Goals embedded in the activities of the Learning Centers may be set up by the children themselves, cooperatively by teacher and children, or by the teacher as he identifies specific needs. The stimulus for setting goals may result from observed growth patterns or demands for enrichment. The actual activity may encourage creative divergence or may involve processes and skills that underlie and underpin fundamental learnings. Meaningful goals established for Learning Centers can utilize behaviorially stated objectives effectively. Behaviorially stated, objectives can present a clear, unequivocal target for the child who is working alone, and the outcome of the activity, i.e., the terminal behavior, may be readily observed and evaluated by both the teacher and the child.

Evaluation of Learning Centers

As a teacher or teacher team develops a more and more comprehensive Learning Center Program, the question of "how am I (or we) doing?" should be faced. Perhaps questions like these will stimulate self-evaluation:

Are the Centers attractive?

Are Centers clear: with respect to goals; and how to get to the goals?

Do the Centers take into account developmental stages of maturity?

Do the children comment that this or that Center is what they were looking for?

Do the children experience a balance between individual activities and group give-and-take?

Do the children have the opportunity to ask for Centers on topics they feel they need?

To answer the above questions, the Learning Center teacher should not attempt to see how much knowledge an individual has gained in comparison to an average or another classmate. The "new Learning Center, teacher" is concerned with elements such as differentiated assignments, differentiated teaching in reference to the individual, large-or small-group instruction, work habits of children . . . . to account for the "elements" in reference to the individual's growth, the teacher needs to devise a form that provides a means for checking on the degree to which the Learning Centers are affecting the progress of the child.

Classification of Learning Centers

Classification structures are quite arbitrary and are usually designed to serve a particular purpose. The approach taken here is to examine Learning Centers actually being used by children to determine their characteristics and then to classify Centers by types which appeared to be operationally useful. The Centers described are not necessarily mutually exclusive but rather represent a focus or an emphasis and while the types that are defined do have overlapping characteristics, they have been selected to provide the teacher with an adequate structure about which to establish a variety of Centers in keeping with the purposes of this "Survival Kit."

INVENTORY LEARNING CENTER. These Centers provide an opportunity to assess the development of the children in arithmetic, reading, problem solving, creativity, etc. Usually an emphasis is placed on this type of Center at the beginning of the school year or when a new student is admitted in order to provide information concerning the appropriate level of work for each child.

Since the classroom teacher usually does not have sophisticated diagnostic materials and procedures at his disposal, this type of Center functions more as an Inventory Center than as a diagnostic center even though the general procedure of collecting data and analyzing it are similar. Actually, most Centers must have diagnostic or inventory procedures associated with them. Professional teachers consistently use the results of work done by children as the basis for meaningful, success-producing follow-up experiences.

At the Inventory Center, the teacher usually arranges for short work periods. After a student has completed the assignment(s), the teacher analyzes the work to determine what the operating level of the child seems to be and what level of work and what type of activity will probably provide for the most growth. A conference with the child at this point can be of great value in helping the teacher and the child establish realistic goals. However, diagnostic procedures are frequently confined to carefully sequenced skills, local curriculum guides, and teachers' manuals valuable resources which can provide the teacher with appropriate sequence structures.

The next step after analysis of the collected information, of course, is to provide a Center activity which will result in the desired learnings. (Section III, page 43 for example).

PRESCRIPTIVE LEARNING CENTER. The work at the Prescriptive Center is a logical outcome of work at the Inventory Center. Use of this type of Center usually presumes a regular, daily work pattern. The level of work and the type of activity are frequently prepared by the teacher alone; however, if a conference between the child and the teacher can become a part of the procedure, the mutual agreement and the resulting commitment can produce results which are unlikely to be achieved otherwise. Local curriculum guides, teacher's manuals, and ideas from the children can be tapped to provide a variety of exciting activities. (See Section III, page 45-46 for example).

PROJECT LEARNING CENTER. In the teacher-made Project Learning Center design, the teacher is the organizer. A "project study guide" is the focal point around which a programmed center is developed and finds its major application in the content areas. The study guide features a major problem with many sub-problems on which the student can elect to work. Second, the problems are primarily open-ended. Third, the study guide for each project has a multi-level activity section, and, finally, a contract arrangement provides for child-teacher planning and evaluation.

A major advantage of the study guide is that it has the potential of offering many options to the student within the Center itself. The student is provided an opportunity to carry the major responsibility for decisions related to planning, executing, and evaluating an area of study.

The teacher, or the Project Center organizer, assesses ahead of time the following:

    a. Interests—individual and total class
    b. Content—appropriate and appealing
    c. Activities—diverse and enticing
    d. Materials—available and relevant

For example, a teacher might program four Centers every six to eight weeks. Four Centers' topics for six weeks might be:

Insects
Microscopes
Electricity
Weather

The student is given a choice of working at one or all of the Centers. After a Center(s) has been selected, choices among sub-topics and activities must also be selected by the student. Care should be taken to ensure that the open-ended sections of the guide provide an array of alternatives, including sub-topics and activities suggested by individual children, so that the interests and abilities of the students can be provided for more adequately. (See Section III, pages 47-54 for example).

PROGRAMMED LEARNING CENTER. This Center utilizes commercially available programmed materials or kits. The teacher obtains a kit from a publisher which he introduces to the children who follow the prescribed program. The kit may provide for cognitive development in a content area or it may emphasize psychomotor activities in a skill development area. Obviously, a thorough understanding of the purpose that the kit is designed to serve, compared with the purpose the teacher has in mind for the Center, is necessary if the investment of money, teacher time, and child time is to be justified.

PROGRAMMED-PROJECT LEARNING CENTER. A combination of the "Project Center" and the "Programmed Center" produces a Center arrangement in which the commercial kit is adapted by the teacher through the medium of a teacher-made project book, multi-level content activities, or assignment sheets designed to meet the assessed needs and interests of the students.

UNIT LEARNING CENTER. A problem area selected by the teacher is the core of the Unit Learning Center. The teacher organizes the Center or Centers around a central theme or separate subject content. The format for the Unit Center, whether central theme or separate subject, reflects the organizational elements of a unit, viz., the use of exposition to attract interest and to stimulate questions, and the use of skill-building activities to acquire information and to develop concepts and generalizations. (See Section III, pages 55-58 for example).

COOPERATIVE LEARNING CENTER. The teacher and student discuss a topic that is of interest to the student. What sets this Center design apart from the other designs is that:

> The discussion with the child starts before the Center has been organized.
>
> The planning and evaluating details, including time limits, are established by the student under the direction of the teacher.
>
> The outcome agreed to by the child and the teacher should be evident at the end of the pre-set period.
>
> (See section III, pages 59-61 and 77-78 for example)

STUDENT LEARNING CENTER. The individual student designs a Center around an interest of his own choice, and shares this interest with the teacher and/or classmates. The dominant feature of this Center is that the individual student establishes objectives and carries forth a planned experience. The teacher assumes a guidance role by responding to the student's request for assistance. One fascinating example of such a Center was one put together by three students titled, "What can you do with a piece of string?"

SKILL DEVELOPMENT LEARNING CENTER. A skill, psychomotor in nature, is a performance or behavior which develops through practice by the learner. A wide variety of skills is demanded by our society and a lengthy sequence of skills can result in a rather complex task. Learning Centers can facilitate the development of single (simple) or multi- (complex) skills by providing appropriate activities that foster their development. The teacher is encouraged to approach this facet of teaching with all the creativity he can muster.

Single Skill Learning Center. These educational task assignments are usually constructed from one content area and require that the student work at a single skill appropriate to his maturational and educational development. It assumes that the child can already perform the task and that the accuracy and efficiency will develop through the practice provided by the activity. The Center can have one task assignment or be open and provide a variety of task assignments to choose from. (See Section III, pages 63-65 for examples).

Multi-Skill. Multi-Skill activities are characterized in the Centers either by their complexity and/or their sequence. Usually the assignments are problem - centered and require the student to use a variety of materials in resolving the question while the major objective remains acquiring proficiency in the skills involved. (See Section III, pages 65-68 for example).

FUN LEARNING CENTER. The Fun Learning Center is modeled after the Interest Center of the 1960's. The teacher is not concerned with identifying the educational task before the student visits the Center and in many situations the learning process is never identified because the educational task is self-imposed and enjoyed without being justified. (See illustration chart on page 12).

COMBINATION LEARNING CENTER. The Combination Learning Center is simply the result of combining the characteristics of two or more previously described Centers into one Center.

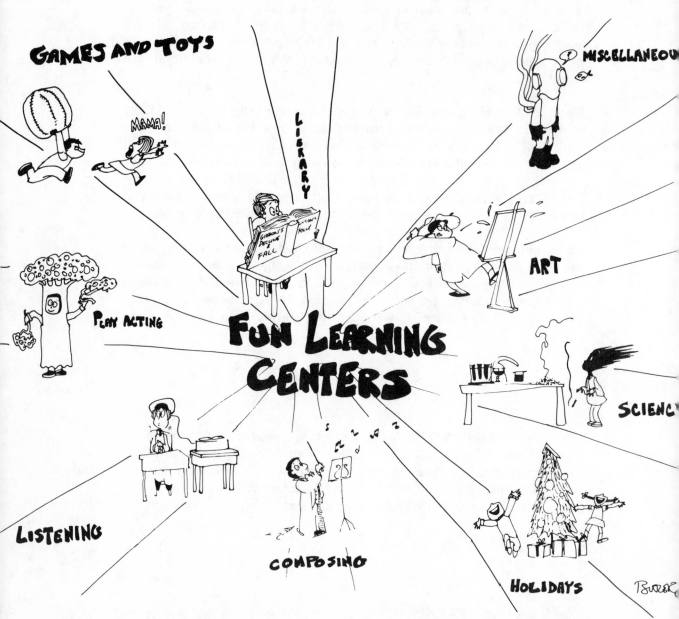

* . . . there are as many Fun Learning Center titles as there are teaching situations.

Before going into a discussion of some of the considerations to be kept in mind when the decision has been made to implement Learning Centers, a general comment seems appropriate.

Learning Centers appear to facilitate some learning and teaching styles more than some other teaching methods. The Learning Center, while it stresses individuality, may nonetheless lead into or grow out of a group activity. Also, while a teacher uses the Learning Center Method, the same teacher may use small group teaching methods as well as total class discussions. It would be presumptuous to suggest that any one method of working with children may be *the* method. So, when a given teacher begins to work concertedly on any given method, he knows that he is selectively planning. He is aware that his action does not imply rejection of all other methods. Realistically, a balance of various techniques seems to be the logical follow-up of the earliest declaration of this book. That is, the preoccupation of the future will be with truly operational individualized classroom procedures because children are unique individuals and have unique personal needs and learning styles.

Teachers Can Change

It seems almost a truism too trite to repeat—teachers want children to succeed. Yet some children fail. Some fail as students; some as persons. What can teachers do?

For some teachers a commitment to a style and a method of teaching may be the answer. The essential idea comes out of the word, COMMITMENT.

The term represents a strong resolve to move toward a goal. The goal—the child's growth, academically and personally.

But goals require means. For some teachers the Learning Center method provides the means. For the teacher who senses a compatibility of personal style of teaching with the method suggested in this "Survival Kit," both the goal and the means are available. But the method that fits *some* teachers means just that. To suggest that any one method fits *all* teachers' styles of teaching would simply imply naiveté.

It is sincerely believed that the Learning Center method holds great promise for those teachers who are in search of a new way to provide for child growth and development and child individuality. That teacher who elects the Learning Center method must be willing to

- work creatively with children's ideas and his own

- utilize a variety of materials—texts, devices (AV and otherwise), kits, and realia

- write and tell directions clearly, precisely, and economically

- settle for nothing less than a comfortable harmony between ideas, facts, and things

- look for progress and success in individuals, as individuals, when evaluating child behavior.

or, if you as the teacher are serious about re-equipping yourself with updated techniques, consider the implications of shifting:

FROM—a course of study to which the child is made to fit

TO—a course of study determined by the needs of the child

FROM—the single-text approach

TO—a multi-media array of materials and information resources , including audio visual resources

FROM—a teaching style which provides abstract symbol activities with the student sitting at his desk with his paper and pencil and/or a question and answer period directed by the teacher

TO—a variety of experiences including 3-dimensional concrete activities with children helping children and moving with self-directed purpose to differentiated assignments at the Centers

FROM—a textbook and telling teacher who gives verbal information

TO—a teacher who is non-directive and guides the student to inquire and to involve himself actively in the process of learning

FROM—separate subject teaching whereby science, history, geography, and spelling are taught at a specific time of day in a narrow conceptual scheme

TO—a gathering of related concepts into an integrated whole through Centers for learning so as to provide a more meaningful experience for the learner

FROM—a teacher who makes assignments and corrects papers

TO—a teacher who cooperatively plans and evaluates the experiences of each child through individual conferences.

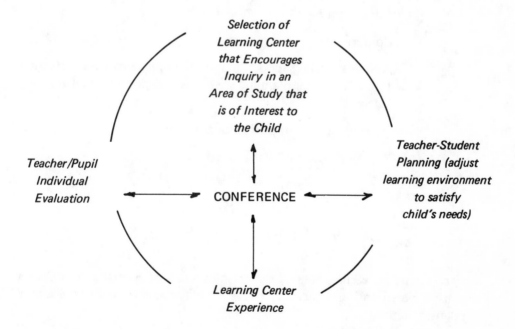

Implementation by the Teacher

Whether one teacher, or a team, or a total staff of teachers, chooses to use the Learning Center method on a limited or all-out basis, each teacher should use every opportunity available to elaborate on the meanings of such ideas as:

What is the meaning of individuality?

How can I bring *ideas* and *materials* together for children?

What is a Center like?

What is a Center classroom like?

Your personal solutions to these questions may be through one or a combination ot the following possibilities:

College course work

Local staff development or in-service workshops

Visitations to schools where the Center method is being used

Consultant help

Conferences

Administrative support that will implement these channels through mutual planning with teachers present at all working levels

Read and study of professional materials

The "Survival Kit" (Devour it!!)

Conversion to Centers

As was suggested earlier, some teachers may convert partially to a Center organized classroom, or some may convert a classroom totally to the Learning Center method.

PARTIAL CONVERSION. A class may use Learning Centers as a part of the learning experience continuum. There may be, for example, a Center for certain skills, there may be a Center for information, there may be one for fun only. The teacher simply uses Centers as supplements, or adjunct techniques, concurrent with some other well-planned program. The teacher may sustain this type of classroom through the entire school year.

Partial conversion permits the teacher to examine some of the implications of Centers. It can provide a profitable relief from the confining limits of assignments and at the same time reveal the positive reactions of children to the self-actualizing potential of Centers.

TOTAL CONVERSION. The teacher uses the Center approach as his dominant organizational arrangement for planning experiences with and for children. Total conversion does not mean Centers exclusively but it does mean that direct teaching by the teacher is subordinated or submerged in favor of self-directed commitments to learning by individual children. The emphasis is on learning rather than on teaching. The no-talk, no-copy pattern of the same text in every child's hands is replaced by the dynamic hum of peers sharing with and helping peers as ideas and information are sorted out of the books, filmstrips, tapes, records, movies, TV, or whatever other source may be expected to provide a profitable yield for the effort and energy expended. Numerous large group meetings will be legitimate, especially for program planning and evaluation purposes. Likewise, common needs of children, especially the younger age groups, may require the frequent formation of small groups to serve numerous legitimate educational ends.

Designing the Center

It is unrealistic to suggest hard rules to follow in putting a Center together. In general, the teacher needs to take into consideration the following categories, in the designing of Centers:

A. An eye-catching, thought-stimulating title that will motivate the child to visit the Center.

B. Pictures and objects that provoke interest and suggest concepts and/or generalizations about areas to be investigated.

C. Guiding questions need to be open-ended so that the child can enter the Center and work at his level and progress to higher levels of learning.

D. In many Centers the reference and activities section is not part of the physical display but grows out of the conference or work project related to the general problem or questions of the Center.

E. Evaluation should be a regular part of the child's experience— teacher conference, or a project workbook.

F. A review of Center examples in Section III indicates that directions need to be clear and an integral part of the design.

Materials for Instruction

There is one novel factor in our times which greatly facilitates individualization and the practical implementation of Centers. That factor is the availability of a diversity of materials which are consistent with developmental levels, learning modes, learning styles, and self-accommodation.

Consider:

Texts
Library books
Programmed instruction
Kits
Slides
Pictures - photographs
Filmstrips
Transparencies
Movies
Cartridge audiotapes
Records
8mm cartridge loops, movie
16mm cartridge loops, movie
Radio
TV
ETV
VTR - video tape recorders
Microfilm
Remote access, retrieval
Telephone (homebound) - dial service
C.A.I. (computer assisted instruction)
Talking typewriter
Copy machines
Overhead projectors
Opaque projectors

Staff

Community specialists

Science equipment

Manipulative materials

Realia

Games

Models

Maps and globes

Art materials

Musical instruments

The list is extensive but not complete. No teacher is likely to have all of these resources available to him or his children, but most schools are acquiring an impressive array of materials and devices, most of which have direct implications for individualization when they are viewed as having the potential.

Children, even older children helping younger children, can select movies and filmstrips and operate the projectors without direct teacher help when given the opportunity and if headsets are available a student can obtain information concerning a project he is working on both auditorily and visually, alone, just as he might read a book, alone.

Or, consider the value of a listening tape as a way to obtain information for a child who can handle vocabulary and concepts beyond his reading ability.

Or, consider the similarity of a student checking out a record and filmstrip from the library resource center as he would a book.

Or, why shouldn't a child check out a record of his own choosing and listen to it alone, just as he would check out a book of his own choosing and read it for pleasure, alone?

Or, consider the values of taping the directions for certain activities, once, and setting up one or many listening posts to be used by many individuals. The materials available to you can enrich your Centers and consequently the lives of your children—if you will:

Survey the materials in your school that you may borrow, or check out.

Shift your thinking from group use of materials and devices to individual use.

Establish a student system for selecting and/or ordering and/ or checking out movie projectors, films, games, etc.

Introduction of Centers

The teacher introducing Learning Centers into the classroom setting needs to be aware that special consideration must be given to the introduction of Centers to children who have never used Centers.

It is difficult to outline one definite method for introducing Centers to a class for the first time because of the existing organizational patterns with which teachers may be confronted. Therefore, several minicase histories of successful classroom transitions to a Center pattern or organization are offered as alternative possibilities.

(1) Double room with no dividing wall. A first and second grade class began school in the fall with the Learning Centers already set up. The teacher, using a brief total class orientation period then introduced the Centers one by one to small groups of children.

(2) Cooperative teaching experiences in separate rooms. Two fourth grade teachers worked with children to develop appropriate attitudes and work habits before using the Center method. The introduction of Centers began with a single Center and grew with new Centers being added from time to time until the entire program was carried on by the Learning Center Teaching Method.

(3) Self-contained sixth grade. After much thought and a great deal of physical preparation, a teacher planned a week's orientation period with the children and then made a complete change to Centers at the beginning of the second week.

(4) Team teaching in separate rooms. The teachers in the team designed the Centers and set them up at the beginning of the school year. The introduction to the Centers consisted of planning and discussion periods during the time normally spent on opening exercises.

Replacing Centers

To replace Centers, after they have served their purpose, the teacher can plan to use the direct approach or indirect approach to remove the old Center and introduce the new one. In the direct approach the teacher is the key agent in exposing the Center to the students. Like a mother hen, she gathers the children around the Center and proceeds to explain. When a teacher uses the indirect approach, the Center is simply made available, the child examines the Center, and then conferences with the teacher about it or if the Center rules allow it, he may simply schedule himself into the Center and questions are resolved through conferences with the teacher and through dialogues with other students.

An essential for all grade levels using the Center approach is that teachers need to think through a plan for their own approach to introducing a Center, whether it be for the first time or for replacing Centers when the need arises.

Child's Free Choice

Significant aspects of the Learning Center method are the early emphasis on child planning for the use of his time and choice of Centers at which to work. At every level, from the youngest to the oldest of children, students must learn how to plan the use of their time. This is accomplished primarily through the use of daily and weekly schedules. (See Section III, pages 69-70 & 75-76).

Centers may have a suggested "time limit" posted. At the same time that this device serves to provide an opportunity to develop skill in budgeting time, the children may use it to help build and maintain a realistic individual schedule. In a person-to-person conference, the child who needs more time gets it, but it does not become a public issue. In the same way, the child who goes too fast—just to get through—is counselled to ease up and do some Centers well and not all Centers poorly.

Choices characterize the Center method:

Choice of Center

Choice of time

Choice of peers

Choice of pace

Choice of interests

While the choice remains an operating emphasis, some teachers do set up required or "must" Centers because the teacher may feel he needs some diagnostic data, or may deem it necessary or desirable to prescribe certain activities to develop specific skills and abilities of some of the students in the classroom.

Choice means simply: picking a task from among alternatives. It may mean picking one or more Centers to do in a given day. It may mean working alone or with a companion. Choice involves inclusion and exclusion. Some things the child elects to do, some to omit. At the same time that free choice receives emphasis in the Center method, the teacher exercises the prerogative of assignment to what may be called "must" Centers. The name, arbitrarily given, may be any term which implies: the teacher guides some children some of the time to specific tasks and choice is not available to the child. This will be developed below.

> In a classroom which has been partially converted to the Center method, choice of Centers may be fairly limited. This is due to the fact that only part of the classroom program has been set up in the form of Centers. Some sort of sign-up method may be used to facilitate indication of choice.

A chart on a wall space accessible to the children listing all the Centers, and the number of working spaces, may be set up. The children may be asked to make their commitment by signing up by name or making an identifying mark of some kind in the proper place on the chart (depending on their maturity). As the working spaces are filled, those Centers are then tempo - rarily closed. Each child is expected to work in the manner pre-set at a planning period. That is, the day he may work, the Centers from which he may choose, and the expectations for accomplishment will have been made clear. Also if he does not complete his commitment satisfactorily, the child may be encouraged or even assigned to return to the same Center the next day. Specific classroom cases will determine local ground rules.

The techniques suggested above seem particularly necessary to set a clear procedure for establishing appropriate expectations for young children. To reiterate, always be sure that optional Centers are available to every child.

Where a classroom has been converted to a total Center Method, choice becomes less limited, but even more significant.

Where Centers are the daily and chief business of the classroom program, the child will be surrounded by Centers of many types. It is his responsibility to select a balanced program. He must learn to use the sign-up system for the class. He must learn to schedule himself by the day and by the week. He learns to choose some Centers for serious business, some from interest alone, and some for fun. He learns how to assist his neighbor who may need help in choosing. He learns how to report through conferences with his teacher, from his own records, what he has planned and accomplished. He learns how to pick up challenges and how to omit them. He learns to live with limits of time, space, wants, and energy.

Young children will require more guidance than will older. All will require some. Older children may work under "contract." That is, they may make a written commitment for a given time period of work. This device specifies and orders his system of choice.

Back to the matter of "must" Centers. Through diagnostic tech- niques, and conferences with the children, the teacher becomes aware of needs in the children. The teacher then assumes in addition to the role of guide, the role of director. He assigns certain Centers (on an individual need basis, person to person). These Centers may deal with drill aspects of instruction. They may require more creative efforts, but choice to omit may not be available. Required Centers may even be "fun" Centers. The essential fact, however, is that the teacher sees a pattern and points it out (clearly and firmly). He then sets the task. In the process of directing, though, an element of freedom may still be kept. This may be done in terms of time to do the job. The child may elect, within limits, how long to take and when to accomplish the "must" Center or Centers.

Record Keeping

In order to ensure that each child is achieving a balance in Center choices, and, therefore, developing the skills and understandings necessary or appropriate for his developmental level, a record of his work must be kept. There are, of course, a number of ways to keep such records. Each teacher, or team, will probably develop his own. Some suggested ways to get started are:

1. A teachers' checklist in a folder combining student names and available Centers can be easily used as a quick daily account of work done or committed.

2. A large chart may be set up on a wall with each child's name placed on it. A star or other symbol for each Center is added by the child's name as he completes his choices. He can then see which Centers are still available to him. This chart may be the same or different from the one on which children declare their choices. As the children develop in their understanding of the chart, they may help to create a variety of symbolic labels which increases involvement.

3. A Center check sheet may be kept at each Center with all children's names listed. As a child works at the Center, he checks his name in the appropriate date column.

4. Each child may keep his own folder, and check, by suitable symbols, that he has done this or that Center. He reports his progress at one of the regular or "called" conferences with the teacher.

5. In order that parents can be kept aware of the kind of work their child is doing, a checklist of each week's work may be sent home together with samples of the child's work. A check or other code might be used to indicate that the work was required, was elective, was required but not completed, or that the Center had been created by the child. The weekly checklist can be an extremely valuable adjunct to the regular report card. (See, also, Reporting to Parents).

Conferences

The type and number of conferences will depend to a large degree on the attitude of the teacher as well as the needs and abilities of the children in the classroom. When Centers are used exclusively, time for conferences is at an optimum. Some basic principles can be outlined which should offer guidance to the teacher as he plans how to incorporate the conference into the total program. Consider these:

1. With the assistance of the students, establish conference rules and procedures.

2. Be consistent in scheduling time for regular conferences.

3. Set up a standard method for recording information during a conference.

4. Prepare a summary statement of the topic discussed for each conference, so that progress of the individual is charted and can be reviewed at a later date.

5. Have a reason for calling any non-routine conferences and reveal the reason to the student involved in the conference.

6. Express positive and supportive comments during each conference so that the child is confronted with an atmosphere that reveals real concern for his personal growth.

There are several types of conferences which commonly take place between pupils and teachers. Some children will require more conferences than others and the teacher is encouraged to establish an atmosphere which fosters these person-to-person exchanges, many of which will be prompted by psychological needs even though the topic discussed may be math.

1. Learning Center Work Conference

   Each child's (folder of) work is evaluated daily. Individual help is given at the conference time. The child's problems and concerns are discussed. During the conference the child and teacher agree on a task or tasks that will promote further growth and success. A very important purpose of the work conference is to find out whether or not the pupil is growing in his understanding of the concepts being developed and in determining what prescriptive work he might need. This type of conference may be brief and take place as often as the child needs one. (See Section III, pages 69-70).

2. Individualized Reading Conference

   At this conference, a careful record is kept of the child's strengths and needs and the progress he is making. The teacher and pupil plan together for the reading selections and the extension of skills either on an individual or small-group basis. *Every* child does not need a reading conference every day with a teacher. On the other hand, *some* children will need to confer daily. (For example, see appendix, pages 71-73).

3. Conference of a General Nature

   This type of pupil-teacher conference can be very valuable in determining a pupil's attitudes, desires, fears, and general classroom adjustment. The pupil should be encouraged to "talk" and the teacher should assume the role of listener. Both can leave the conference with a better understanding of each other and the school.

4. Report Card Conferences

   The real substance of the report card conference supposedly brings about a mutual understanding of the abstract symbol. Any grading symbols are interpreted through a discussion of the activities which have been provided and which have been engaged in by the child. The child should know as far in advance as practical that the report card conference has been scheduled.

This knowledge allows the child to evaluate his folder and to complete commitments which he wishes to include in the evaluation.

The conference as it relates to reporting is developed further in the next section.

Reporting

One of the more difficult adjustments which the teacher may have to make may be in the area of arriving at a mark to be recorded on a report card. The mark on a report card should be an outgrowth of the numerous conferences between the teacher and the student. The conferences provide the opportunity for collecting information for the grade mark. During a conference prior to the end of the grading period, the teacher and student weigh the result of the child's efforts and reach an agreement concerning the quality and quantity of the work done by the student and together establish a grade based on growth.

In many classrooms the teacher and student can prepare separate report cards and then compare grades, or progress statements, with the teacher having the right of posting the final symbol on the report card.

A teacher who is concerned about maintaining a positive self-image for students may find a modified criterion-referenced system of some value. It is possible, for example, for a sixth grade student functioning on a fourth grade level to receive something more than a failing grade. Either comments, or a letter grade, with a number behind the letter indicating the grade level, might be used to communicate with all interested parties the kind of achievement the student is making during a particular grading period. The double symbol system can allow a student to work at an appropriate level without supporting a try-fail-frustration syndrome.

    Example

English	C_4
Mathematics	B
Reading	C_4

Reporting to Parents

The assumption has been made that most teachers considering the question of reporting must use some type of the A, B, C, etc. system. Teachers working in systems which do not employ this system have a distinct advantage when it comes to reporting. Since this is true, emphasis is placed on reducing the problems presented by letter grades.

It is very difficult for a parent, who may read a letter grade at the end of a reporting period, to obtain an adequate interpretation of the symbol. Since progress and achievement of the individual is the message, the teacher needs to design an educational program for the parents so that the grade that represents many learning acts by the child will carry a deeper meaning than just a letter representing a relative position on a scale. The following are just a few of the lead-up reports that will lend meaning to the symbol:

1. A folder sent home for parents to review, initial, and return to school.

2. A telephone conversation.

3. A school conference with parents (in many situations the child should be included in the conference).

4. A selection of Center activities that include the parent in the learning process.

5. An open-door visitation policy.

6. A parent-aide program that involves the parents in classroom functions.

Time-Saving Measures

Does a teacher spend *more time* at home designing Learning Centers than the time normally spent on a resource unit and all the related activities to a unit?

For the first month apparently the time spent preparing Centers is approximately double the time spent on writing a resource unit and planning related unit activities. As the teacher gains experience in constructing Centers, the time needed to prepare Centers is decreased greatly.

Many factors account for the decrease of time spent on the construction of Centers. After a teacher understands what the Learning Center approach to teaching is, specific time-saving measures just seem to develop. Some of the general time-saving measures that can be planned for are outlined below:

- Interest and Needs in Relation to Center Design

    While the teacher is finding out about the interests and needs of a student he should be aware of the Center designs described and how they apply to the individual in question. Once a teacher is able to match interest and needs to the Centers, without hesitating, time will be saved. This time-saving process might be called *Creative Center Design*.

Creative Design is a process whereby the teacher observes a child at work in the Learning Center environment to determine what type of Center design and content best suits him. The possibilities generated by these observations are then discussed in conference. Somewhere on the conference form the teacher should make notes concerning the Center design to be used next for a student (or a group of students).

- Student Routines in Relation to Center Management

    The student must know how to respond to the different Center designs. Therefore, routines must be fostered so that the student can become increasingly autonomous while working at a variety of Centers.

The time spent on correcting or leading the children through the Centers can be spent more profitably in conferencing with students.

- Parent Aides in Relation to Center Activity

    Not only can the parent be used in doing the housekeeping jobs, and putting Centers together, but she can be used to act as a *feedback agent*.

Parent aides, as a feedback agent, can be expected to interact with a child in a general manner such as:

(a) reading directions

(b) asking leading questions that start the child to think: "Would you explain to me what the teacher wants you to do while working at this Center?"

(c) assisting the child in spelling a word

(d) monitoring

(e) having a key to correct a written exercise before the teacher conferences with the child.

(f) allowing a child to verbalize aloud (practice before a conference with a teacher).

(g) typing creative stories dictated by the student

● Teacher arranges an overall schedule for the construction of new Centers

After the teacher establishes techniques for designing Centers, the next step is to develop a master plan for replacing Centers with new ones.

A very realistic system for replacing Centers is to develop a schedule so that at no time are all the Centers replaced on one day of the week. A general plan might be to replace two Centers on Monday and Wednesday or three on Friday—the main point being that a teacher should not attempt to replace all Centers on the same day.

● Coding Centers Saves Time

Coding of the Centers is very important so that the code and Center title when stated flashes an image in the teacher's mind.

The signal given by a number code can carry along with it the purpose of the Center and related information. The number or number series of a Center should be assigned an area of study for an extended period of time.

Example:

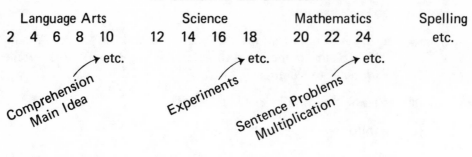

20 Centers in the Classroom

Language Arts	Science	Mathematics	Spelling
2 4 6 8 10	12 14 16 18	20 22 24	etc.

Comprehension
Main Idea

Experiments

Sentence Problems
Multiplication

At first this rather rigid numbering of Centers might seem very formal. In the long run the numbering of Centers not only gives guidance to the child and the teachers, but it is also a time-saving device whenever questions are asked that require an immediate response about the Centers in the classroom.

- Coordination of Instruction Materials and Devices into Center Formats

  At first, it is hard and time consuming to think of different ways materials and devices can best be used in learning situations.

As time passes, and experiences multiply, the Learning Center teacher realizes the student is quite capable of handling materials and manipulating devices independently.

Furniture Usage

Your first impulse may be to draw pictures to illustrate how furniture can be moved to provide large work areas for children to occupy. The moving of furniture into different pattern designs is important but the Learning Center teacher needs to go beyond this stage of thinking and develop ways to incorporate classroom furniture and instructional items into the Center design so as to enhance the learning opportunity for the individual.

The following sketches with a brief comment have been included to illustrate how the classroom furniture and instructional items can be utilized when constructing a Center:

Any desk figure arrangement can be designed when using student desks. In order to provide area space for Center displays, desks can be arranged with a large piece of plywood covering the desks.

wooden & cork cross stand

A variety of arrangements with filing cabinets and student tables can be contrived.

art easels

construction paper attached onto chalkboard edge

chart rack

portable blackboard

bookcase-portable blackboard

the folding and pasting of three sheets of poster board to construct a center divider

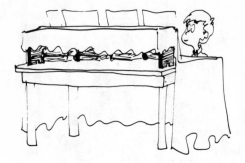

The large table with a bench or small table on top of large table makes a complete Center within itself. The front can be used for display and the area under the small table or bench can be used for storage.

Corrugated cardboard and student desks can be used in the middle of a room or in any area where it is impossible to construct a Center near a wall.

LOCAL GOVERNMENT

YE OLDE PEEP SHOW

The teacher's desk can be used as a screen area.

For the Learning Center teacher the day of trial and error in placing furniture to obtain storage of apparatus and materials is passe. Each teacher develops techniques for contriving furniture usage patterns into Center format.

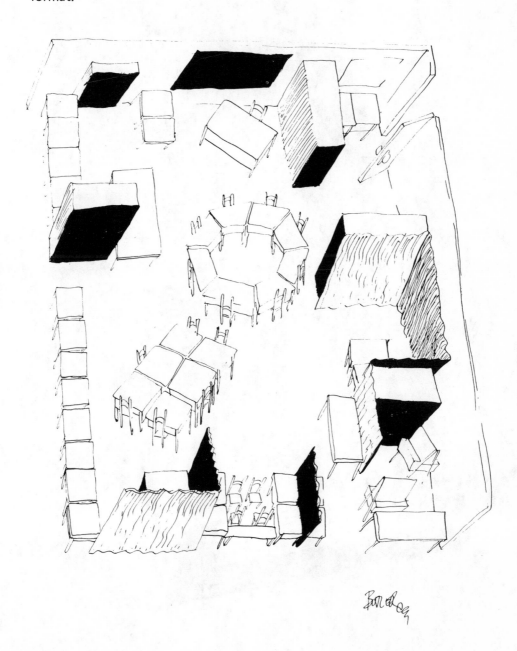

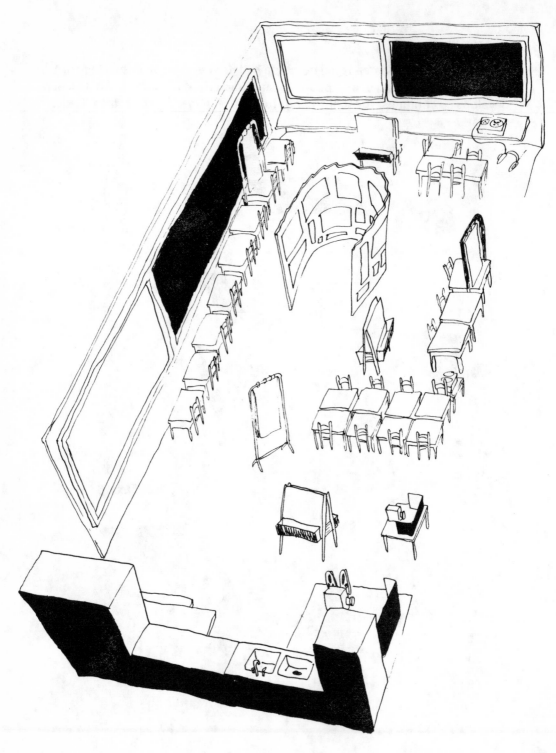

INVENTORY LEARNING CENTER

Educational Task:

to discover what each youngster knows about the letters of the alphabet.

Materials:

(a) Large card of manuscript alphabet letters (3 letters on each card).
(b) Wide-lined writing paper
(c) Sharp pencils
(d) Clear, simple directions on a chart, asking the child to reproduce the letters correctly (read the directions with the child).

Aa   Bb   Cc

Directions:

A   B   C's

1. Do you know the names of the ABC's? Can you write the ABC's?

2. Take a card. Look at the letters. Say their names to a buddy.

3. On your paper copy the 3 letters.

4. Do this on 4 rows.

5. Write your name on your paper.

PRESCRIPTIVE LEARNING CENTER

Educational Task: Solve problems and equations in simple addition:

After carefully inventorying the students, teachers then set up Centers in those areas of the curriculum where the children are weak, and where self-growth can be attained. The learning should be differentiated at each Center in order to meet individual needs and interests.

An example of a prescriptive Learning Center at the primary level:

Materials:

(a) An individual bag of color-coded math rods for each child.

(b) A work paper with incomplete equations or a reasoning problem to be solved using the rods. Each child discovers the correct answer or solution to the problems by experimenting with the rods. This helps him gain automatic control of number facts, which is one of the mathematic goals.

Display area:

Boy and girl using math rods and making general statements. Some of these same statements can be recorded on a tape recorder. Along with the picture of the boy and girl would be the following numbers and words:

MATH RODS

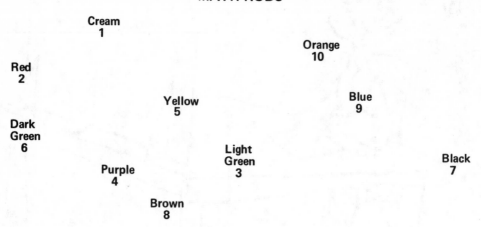

Cream
1

Orange
10

Red
2

Yellow
5

Blue
9

Dark
Green
6

Light
Green
3

Black
7

Purple
4

Brown
8

Directions:

1. Take a bag of rods.

2. Do you know how much each rod stands for? Find the rods.

3. Look at your paper.

4. Find the answers to your equations or problems with the rods.

5. Write your answers like this: 5 + 3 = 8

    yellow + light green = brown

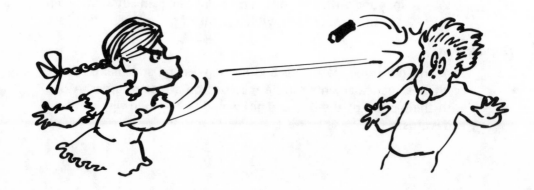

PROJECT LEARNING CENTER

Here is your booklet that will guide you as you use this Center.

The topic is Simple Chemistry related to Ocean Water. This is a part of the larger topic, Oceanography.

Examine the booklet first.

Work with the initial experience—(note the materials available).

Make a contract with your teacher to do some follow-up work.

Best to you.

A PERSONAL INVENTORY

(Comment, in writing, on one or both of the following. Work on whichever part you think fits your needs best).

I want to know more about chemistry because:

I already know the following about chemistry:

BEGINNING EXPERIENCES

The objective of the Center is to allow the child to test some unknown solids (in powder or lump form) to see if they will dissolve in water at room temperature. In addition to three (3) panels, see drawing, the teacher (alone or assisted by a child or committee) provides the following:

1. Four solids (listed here) in numbered but unnamed containers (about 5 or 6 ounces of each):

> table salt
> corn starch
> dry clothes starch
> baking soda

2. Pint or quart of water in pour-spout plastic jar (well rinsed bleach bottle with handle).

3. For each child: Four (4) small size baby food jars, marked at one ounce level.

4. A half-teaspoon measure with each solid.

5. Sheet cake pan.

6. Procedure sheets.

Procedure Sheet

1. Take 4 bottles

2. Place them in the tray before you

3. Put one level measure of solid (powder)* in each bottle—as in this diagram:

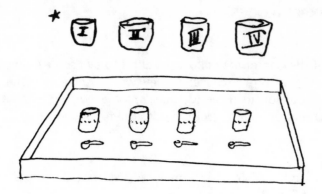

4. Add water to each jar (up to the mark)

5. Make up a sheet on which to record what happened and to use to report your work

6. The following may be useful:

   a. Which solid (powder) dissolved? Which did not?

   b. What (may) help(s) the process of dissolving?

   c. Would dissolving work better if the solid (powder) were *added* to water, not water on top of solid? How can you test this?

   d. In what way does time play a part in dissolving?

CONTRACT FOR MORE STUDY ON SIMPLE CHEMISTRY

(Things that Dissolve)

Here are topics related to the activity you just completed at the Center. These are additional investigations for you to explore. With these projects you will extend your knowledge and understanding.

1. Try the same four (4) solids or powders in rubbing alcohol. How well do they dissolve? Keep records so you can compare with water.

2. Repeat #1, but use vinegar. Compare again.

3. Then repeat #'s 1 and 2, but use soapy water.

4. What would happen if you now return to using plain water, but first heat it? It's not necessary for the water to be boiling, just hot to the touch. (How about *very cold* water?)

5. Now you may wish to add some powdered solids to your list: cocoa, flour, sugar, confectioner's sugar, boric powder, talcum, gypsum.

6. Now test the question of how much. How much salt or sugar will dissolve in a certain amount of water? Begin with an ounce of water (room temperature). Add a teaspoon of salt or sugar at a time. Stir until dissolved. Count how many spoons full will dissolve in the water until no more will dissolve. What might be done to the water to get it to dissolve even more? Salt or sugar?

7. Take 2 or 3 ounces of water. Dissolve 3 or 4 teaspoons full of sugar in it. Pour this solution into a shallow pan or dish. After some hours what happens? How does this help you think about getting solids out of water? How can you save the water?

8. Get some filter paper. Line the top part of a funnel with the filter paper. (Wet the paper first, it will fit more easily into the funnel). Make a few ounces of muddy water. Place the funnel into a jar. Pour some of the muddy water into the funnel top. Compare what's left of the muddy water with what comes

through the filter paper. How does the filtered water differ from other solutions? What would happen if you allowed some of the filtered water to evaporate?

Suggested Questions Related to Simple Chemistry: (Chemistry of Ocean Water)

What kinds of solutions are there?

What materials dissolve earliest?

What materials take other things into solution best?

What conditions help things dissolve?

What is the source of the water and the chemicals in the seas?

How does the ocean water chemistry affect the living things found in it?

How does ocean water affect ships and boats?

How is ocean water different from fresh water to the swimmer?

What gases may be found dissolved in ocean water?

What happens to the remains of animals and plants that die in the ocean?

Bibliography

A bibliography is to be kept throughout this project listing all sources of information including books, films, periodicals, filmstrips, etc.

CONTRACT: A written agreement between child and teacher in which the child declares what he will do, how soon, and in what way.

CONTRACT FOR THE STUDY OF THE SIMPLE CHEMISTRY OF OCEAN WATER

The following are additional work topics in each of the listed areas. When you have completed your selection from these areas of study, all topics must be submitted for contract with the teacher.

Additional topics for investigation (that you think of on your own) may be submitted to the teacher so that records are kept in order to keep the teacher informed of your plans and progress.

Vocabulary

From your readings, develop a vocabulary list of words and their meanings related to ocean water chemistry, such as, salt solution, brine.

Visual

Label and color graphs, drawings or diagrams of the kinds of chemicals that can be found in the oceans and their uses. Example, iodine (a strong dissinfectant—not to use on skin).

Problems and Activities

Solve the suggested problems by performing the accompanying suggested activities. Upon completing these activities, you will have gained enough background information to draw your own scientific conclusions to the problems presented.

Projects

a) Construct a salt water aquarium. Keep a day by day account of all conditions, observations, and findings.

b) Stock with tiny seahorses or other ocean water life. Observe and report on progress and behavior.

ACTIVITIES AND INFORMATION RELATING TO
SIMPLE CHEMISTRY (OCEAN WATER)

Study the life cycle of two plants from the ocean and tell how they benefit from the ocean chemicals in the water.

Study the life and behavior of two kinds of ocean animals that have no backbone and relate their ways to the ocean world. Example: Octopus, Sea Anemone.

Make a diorama of undersea life.

Make a collection of accounts of hurricanes and their relationship to the oceans and the water itself.

Make a shell collection (marine only). What chemicals make up shells?

Make a book about sharks.

Set up a demonstration of how to get fresh water from salty ocean water.

Find out about bouyancy. How does the addition of dissolved things change bouyancy?

UNIT LEARNING CENTER
Develop Generalization about Space

Center #1—Motivation and Introduction

In Center One the teacher reproduces the so-called motivation and classroom introduction phases of a unit into a very charming display for the student to indulge in. Usually the activity at this Center is of a general nature and does not require the student to involve himself in a lengthy activity.

CENTER DISPLAY AREA

Display of space pictures with generalization statement or question beside a picture.

Picture (s)

Record and listening post
Books on display
Movie
etc.

Generalization expressed

Ancient people have marveled at heavens. Man's concept of space has ranged from the superstitious, religious, through early scientific explanations to present-day super-scientific fields of knowledge.

What is meant by *space all around us?*

The content of the movie, books, and records provides the facts and motivation for the student . . . as he examines . . . the topic, space.

Allow a section of the bulletin board for the student to write generalization as they examine the materials at the Center.

As the teacher conferences the student or small groups he must be contriving situations so that the individuals who need to visit all the Centers do so. It is not mandatory to have a student visit all the Centers related to the topic. The teacher can organize the Unit Learning Center to work in a series or Independent Centers with the students only working at one Center.

Center #2 —Activity

This Center usually features the activity part of a unit. The student is allowed to select an activity to express what he has learned about space while at Center #1. In some situations, the student is interested enough to think of his own activity and does not have to select an activity from the Center.

Either hang from the ceiling or stand on a table a general list of activities the student can choose to express what he has learned about space. Some activity examples are:

1. Make a space travel glossary.

2. Construct a who's who of space travel.

3. Draw cut-out views of rockets.

4. Make a chart showing how space exploration affects man.

5. Make a diorama of a launching pad.

6. Design a bulletin board to show how many people are involved when a space shot takes place.

Center #3—Evaluation or test

This Center can represent the evaluation phase of a unit. The teacher or even students can prepare tests on space, after which the students in the class are allowed to select a ditto test paper and shine forth knowledge learned at the space centers in the room.

Centers #'s 4, 5, 6—Skill or skills that need to be developed

Like any other unit the teacher might feel that an individual or groups of students need to practice a particular skill or skills so the teacher uses a high interest area (space) to practice a skill. Some general areas for constructing Centers around are:

Outlining

Before writing a creative story about space-flight, outline the major categories you are going to include in the story.

Spelling   Change the following space vocabulary words from singular to plural (be sure to use plural word in sentence)

. . .

(Music and Art are two other areas that the teacher can use for Center 4.)

COOPERATIVE LEARNING CENTER—GRADE 1 AND/OR 2

Educational Task — Student Creative Thought

This type of Center can be most exciting for children. Here, they can "pre-tend" to the point that they lose themselves in "their world." It is helpful to semi-structure their thinking, that is, to get them started by giving them a choice of starting lines and interest areas to write about. A discussion of the subject and an interchange of ideas with the children is a "must." This way, the child who has no thought of his own can "borrow" his friend's ideas (freely contributed) to get him started. This example of a Center, given here, uses a live bird—one of the class pets. The animal at another time might be a hamster, a turtle, a silkworm, a fish, a butterfly, or a snail. Plants or hats in a child's world may provide inspiration or another occasion when developing a Cooperative Learning Center.

"The World of Feathers"

Center Work Area　　　　　*Materials:*

    a. writing paper

    b. pencils

    c. crayons

    d. drawing paper

Charts for Center

    A. Questions to guide thinking

    B. important facts about birds

    C. Interesting words about birds

    D. Kinds of birds

    E. Directions and activity for the student

Examples of Charts

Chart A *(Questions to guide children's thinking)*

Questions to help you think:

1. What is a bird?

2. What do you know about Perky—class pet?

3. Have you ever had a bird for a pet?

4. Do you like birds?

5. Would you like to pretend you were a bird?

Chart B
(Important Facts)

Birds have:

2 wings
2 legs
feathers
a bill
a home
habits
air sacs

Chart C
(Interesting words about birds)

Bird Words:

nests	plummage
eggs	flies
chirping	sky
swooping	rests
seeds	pecks
sings	peeps
feeds	hops

Chart D (Kinds of birds)

robin	bluejay	cardinal
barnswallow	bobwhite	Baltimore oriole
whipporwill	dove	blue birds
wren	humming bird	crow

Chart E

1. Look at Perky
2. Read Charts A and B
3. Use as many "Bird Words" as you can.

Activity—Direction would be together on one chart

Assignment for each child would vary—differentiated assignments based on interest and needs. In general, the children would work at the Center and record their story about birds in general or about Perky the class pet into the tape recorder. The teacher or parent aides would type the story while the child draws a picture to illustrate the story. The story and picture would be displayed in the classroom.

For the child who might need the experience of printing the story (writing lesson), the teacher would have him copy the typed story and display the child's written work next to the picture on a bulletin board.

SINGLE SKILL
Using Commas

Definition of comma. . .

Pictures of Mother, Father, Child preparing to go to the beach or at the beach.

Directions:
Place a comma where one is needed. How many commas did you use?

_____

Activity Chart Work

1. Robbie said "I'm going to the beach."
2. Joanna said "Is your father going?"
3. Ralph asked "Where are we going?"
4. Mother went to the beach today.
5. Ralph exclaimed "I'm here!"

SINGLE SKILL
Using Exact and Specific Verbs

Picture:

Space Pictures

General information

In writing stories the writer has many possible choices of action verbs. The word *went* has many action verbs that can be used in its place. Read the sentence below.

The space ship *went* into orbit this morning.

As a mental exercise, read the above sentence and replace *went* with each of the verbs listed below:

List A	List B	List C
stormed	slipped	tottered
crawled	inched	
blasted	dashed	

Activities

1. Can you add to List C of action verbs? Record your action verbs on the 5 x 7 cards.

2. In several days a space ship will return to earth. Write sentences to describe the ship's flight as it returns to earth.

Note: *As the teacher conferences with the student, the activity section of the Center can be expanded into a different Center type—Multi-skill, Unit center, Cooperative Center. The needs and interest of the class is the deciding factor if the Skill Center is to be expanded.*

MULTI-SKILL LEARNING CENTER

Solve a problem and use research skills

A Multi-Skill Center should provide an opportunity for children to become acquainted with and to use a variety of research materials and techniques in order to obtain information and to coordinate and state it in a logical and orderly manner.

Materials employed include encyclopediae, dictionaries, (both English and foreign language), all types of books—music, story, history, geography,—maps, newspapers, magazines, pamphlets, almanacs, graphs, and tables.

Techniques in using these materials involve the use of the index and table of contents, thorough knowledge of alphabetization, use of guide words in dictionaries and encyclopediae, understanding of cross references, ability to read map legends and symbols, knowledge and use of diacritical marks, and, most important of all, being able to screen the material read for the relevant facts needed for the solution of the research problem.

One device which has been used is called the "Sleuth Booth." This was initiated with a sign which read—"Calling all detectives! This week's mystery—What is the connection between Mary Had a Little Lamb and Thanksgiving? Watch here for clues."

The clues were printed in white on black footprints and presented on a day.

> Clue #1: Look up Godey, Louis Antoine, in the G volume of the encyclopedia.
>
> Clue #2: Using the cross-reference for Godey, find your next clue.
>
> Clue #3: Look up *Thanksgiving* in the encyclopedia.
>
> Clue #4: Coordinate your clues and write your solution.

The facts obtained from Clue #1 were that Godey had published a magazine and Sarah Hale was the editor.

Clue #2—The cross-reference of Sarah Hale provided the information that she wrote "Mary Had a Little Lamb."

Clue #3 — In the article on Thanksgiving the fact emerged that because of Sarah Hale's urging, Lincoln proclaimed Thanksgiving as a national holiday. Following is a third-grader's responses to the problem:

"Godey founded the Ladies Magazine. Hale, Sarah Josepha, was an editor and author. She was editor of the Ladies Magazine and later she was the editor of Godey's Lady Magazine for fifty years. She wrote the beloved children's poem, "Mary Had a Little Lamb." She wanted Abraham Lincoln to make Thanksgiving Day a national holiday."

Other "mysteries" and solutions by third graders are:

Mystery: What is the connection between Thunder and Lightning and Christmas.

Solution: Thunder and Lightning have to do with Christmas because Santa's two last reindeer are Donner and Blitzen. Donner means thunder and blitzen means lightning. This also has to do with Clement Moore because he wrote the poem "Twas the Night Before Christmas." And he used these names, Donner and Blitzen, to show that these two reindeer were awfully powerful.

Mystery: What is the connection between the state of Maryland and Christmas?

Solution: The first country that decorated trees for Christmas was Germany. "Tannenbaum" in German means "a fir tree." There is a Christmas song that is about a fir tree: "O, Christmas Tree." The state song of Maryland is set to the tune of this song of fir trees.

Mystery: What is the connection between Tchaikovsky and Clement Moore?

Solution: Peter Ilyich Tschaikovsky wrote, conducted, and composed "The Nutcracker Suit." In his story he mentioned the sugarplum fairy in "The Night of Sweets." In Clement Moore's poem, "Twas the Night Before Christmas" the children had visions of sugarplums in their heads.

The "mystery" has to be so worded that the solution cannot be guessed. There must be at least three to five "clues" leading to the final solution. Until the last clue is explored the answer to the problem must be impossible. This requires careful wording of both the "mystery" and the "clues." The clues should be varied enough to allow for the use of many kinds of materials.

As the children become more adept in the use of reference materials, the "clues" will become less detailed and the problems more complex.

Accurate solutions, neatly written, correctly spelled, and clearly and logically stated earn a badge labeled "Super Sleuth." The first one to submit a correct solution merits a star on the badge. The badges—of yellow construction paper—are pinned to the papers as they are returned.

This method of stimulating reference work emerges as a "fun type" project, entered into with enthusiasm and a rush to see each clue as it is posted in the morning.

An approach to the use of dictionary skills which involve the use of guide words, diacritical marks, discrimination in the choice of definition and thorough knowledge of alphabetization is through a Center called "The Aviary." There is a sign which says "You can be a word bird if you can draw and pronounce" and three sets of words are posted. These are changed weekly and only one is required.

Examples of sets of words:

      a lachrymose damsel (weeping girl)

      a flexuous thoroughfare (a winding highway)

      a riant equine (a laughing horse)

      an alate pachyderm (a winged elephant)

Fun, dictionary skills, and art can all be combined in this Center.

CENTER WORK CONFERENCE*

	Yes	No

Did you receive help at the Center from a

       Parent

       Child

       Teacher

Did you find the project

       easy

       difficult

       just right

       interesting

Did you begin your work as soon
as you reached the Center?

Are you proud of your work?

       neatness

       completed

       best writing

       original thoughts

Have checked Center work for

       Spelling

       Capital Letters

       Punctuation

       Complete Sentences

       Content

Is there an idea you could contribute to the
Center?

       Comment:

Have you any suggestions for future Center work?

       Comment:

*This type of form may be used at all grades. The form may be modified depending on the developmental level of the children in a particular situation.

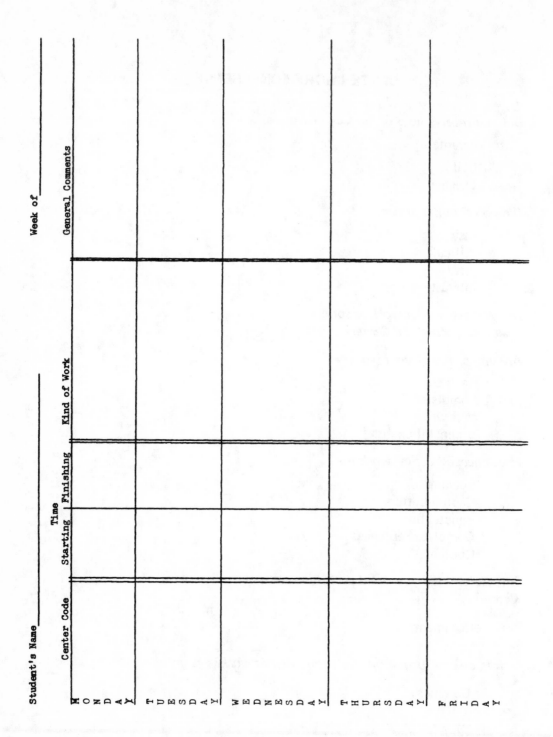

Student's Name _____

Week of _____

	Time			
Center Code	Starting	Finishing	Kind of Work	General Comments
MONDAY				
TUESDAY				
WEDNESDAY				
THURSDAY				
FRIDAY				

INDIVIDUALIZED READING CONFERENCE FORM

Before reviewing the actual form, the teacher needs to have a knowledge of the three levels or stages that are a basic part of the form. The actual form can be 5 x 8 cards, pages in a notebook, or loose sheets that are prepared in advance by some duplicating system.

Initial level

On the conference form the teacher records the following:

Name of student

Date of conference

Level of book

Name of book read from

Medial level

In an appropriate place the teacher records information about the reading progress of the student. The following are general categories and questions that need to be considered when conferencing a student:

1. *Comprehension*
   a. How well does the child retell the story?
   b. How can he tell who are main characters?
   c. How did the story begin?
   d. What happened next?
   e. How did the story end?
   f. How well does the child use vocabulary from the story?

2. *Take an oral sample:*
   a. How many words did the child miss?
   b. What skill does the child need?
   c. Does the child phrase the sentences smoothly as he reads?
   d. Does the child's use of expression suggest that he senses meaning in the words?

71

Final level

The teacher guides the student into the next level of work and records the information on the form. Some prescriptive questions that need to be considered are:

a. Which skills should be reviewed?

b. What new skills will be presented?

c. What educational task or activity should be assigned as practice for the child?

d. How can the teacher assess the most useful materials for this child?

e. What materials are on hand?

f. How best to use many media for the child's greatest potential for progress?

EXAMPLE OF INFORMATION RECORDED

Side one of conference sheet (Medial Level)

Mar. 13	Friends of Ours	Basal 2^2
April 13	Airplanes	Science 3^1 (too hard)
April 13	How to Fly an Airplane	Science 2^2

Side two of conference sheet (Final Level)

March 13 to page 13 (handling easily) missed *neighborhood*. Worked on root words and endings. Gave paper to do on root words.

March 14 checked paper. O.K. top 20. Very good oral. Missed *undercover*. worked on compound words (assign. 20-25. 5 compound words).

March 15 (assign. O.K.) to page 32. Very good oral. phonic paper on "er" ending to nouns.

Individualized Reading Form

1. **Name**   **Date**

   Book

   Approximate level of book

2. Medial level data

   a.

   b.

   c.

Reading form (reverse side)

3. Final level

   a.

   b.

   c.

A Primary Schedule Might Include:

9:30 Pupil-teacher planning for the day. Pupil commitments for Center work Sharing—NEWS—Group interactions

10:00 Silent reading at Centers—Teacher is free (1) to circulate, (2) to conference, (3) to work with small groups explaining Center work, (4) to present new skills to small groups or individuals.

10:30 (1) Individuals work at the Centers.

(2) Clusters of children go to browse in the library.

(3) Teacher confers with individual children or small groups.

(4) Parent aides help children at the Centers.

(5) Parent aides act as secretaries for recording and typing dictated stories.

11:30 P.E.

11:48 Lunch

12:15 Storytime

12:30 Individual pursuit in math, with teacher working with small groups and individuals.

1:30 Group work in spelling skills with individualized enrichment activities.

2:00 P.E.

2:30 Teacher works with group in pursuing science or social studies skills.

3:00 Evaluation—individual group

SIMPLE DAILY SCHEDULE
(Two teacher team)

9:30 - 9:45	Opening exercises, lunch count, general notices
9:45 - 10:00	Individual Center planning by students—the teacher is a consultant
10:00 - 11:00	Individualized reading conferences and peak lesson instruction

Teacher 1	*Teacher 2*
4 individual conferences	6 individual conferences
10 general question answers	5 visits to centers
1 peak math lesson	10 general questions answers
2 visits to centers	2 peak spelling lessons

(Peak lesson size ranges from 8-15 students)

11:00 - 11:15	Recess break
11:15 - 12:10	Center work conferences Small, large group instruction
12:10 - 12:40	Lunch
12:40 - 1:00	Story hour
1:00 - 1:20	Center work conferences Individual reading conferences
1:20 - 1:50	P.E.
1:50 - 2:30	Social Studies period (Center work, etc.)
2:30 - 3:10	Art peak lesson and Center work
3:00 - 3:20	Clean-up, evaluation, and dismissal

The same general pattern is used in large team organizational pattern and in the self-contained classroom organizational pattern.

COOPERATIVE LEARNING CENTER

Educational Task: To provide opportunity for child to understand economics and use of money in everyday living.
Area: Math
Levels: (Primary: 6, 7, 8, 9 yr. olds)
Materials: (a) Actual food containers to display at Center
(b) Charts and student work sheet (see below)

CHARTS:

(DIRECTION CHART I)

Follow these directions

1. Take a paper from Easy or Hard
2. Read the shopping story
3. Use the tax chart
4. Solve the problem
5. Draw the number picture
6. When you finish one, try another story

CHART II (TAX)

How much tax do I pay?

Amount of sale	Tax
1c-14c	No tax
15c-34c	1c
35c-59c	2c
60c-84c	3c
85c-$1.14c	4c

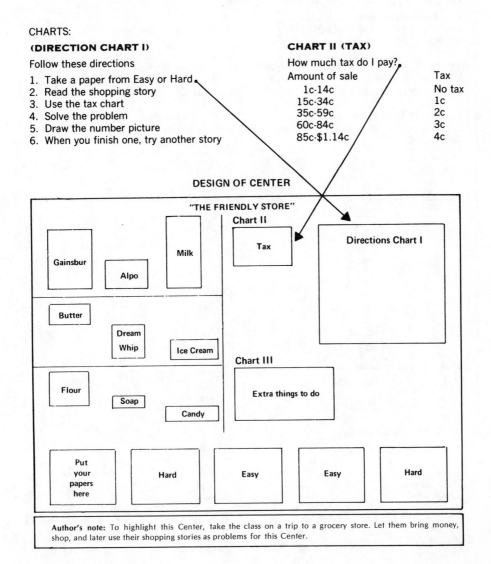

DESIGN OF CENTER

"THE FRIENDLY STORE"

Chart II

Gainsbur

Alpo

Milk

Tax

Directions Chart I

Butter

Dream Whip

Ice Cream

Chart III

Flour

Soap

Candy

Extra things to do

Put your papers here

Hard

Easy

Easy

Hard

Author's note: To highlight this Center, take the class on a trip to a grocery store. Let them bring money, shop, and later use their shopping stories as problems for this Center.

CHART III (EXTRA WORK)

At the Store:

It is fun to shop.
You need money.
You must look at the prices on each box or can.
You must remember the tax.
Look carefully at your check.

1. For fun make up a store check.
2. Add up the items.
3. Add the tax.
4. Total the check.

Samples of Easy and Hard student worksheets:

EASY WORKSHEET

John's mother wanted to make cookies. She went to buy butter and Dream Whip. What was her check? What was the tax?

Jane went to the store. Her dog Nippy needed food. She bought Gainesburgers and Alpo. How much did she spend? How much tax did she pay?
Spencer bought three cans of chocolate pudding. Each cost 27c. What did the cans cost?

HARD WORKSHEET

At the store Barbara spent 39c on candy. Each piece cost 13c. How many pieces of candy did she buy? Did she pay any tax?

DESIGN OF CENTER

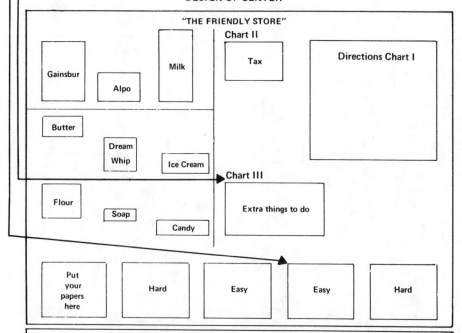

Author's note: To highlight this Center, take the class on a trip to a grocery store. Let them bring money, shop, and later use their shopping stories as problems for this Center.

Invention — Not Learning Center Traditions

Learning Center teaching is beginning to switch from a Learning Center traditional state of affairs to Learning Center inventions to understand methodology. For a long time educators have been passing on the following traditions about Learning Centers without questioning.

> Learning Center design is the teachers' thing!
> Creativity is the core of Center teaching!
> In order to do Learning Centers the teacher does her thing!
> A teacher must observe Learning Centers in order to use
> Learning Centers!

Invention is used to mean the questioning of the Learning Center classroom environment for teacher/learner improvement. Teachers are no longer accepting the above truths or traditions but rather adjusting classroom situations so that Learning Center teaching depends on methodology and artistry. Some of the areas teachers are analyzing and inventing so as to understand Center teaching are:

> Definition of Centers
> Vocabulary usage
> Classification
> Models
> Implementation procedures
> Instructional material usage
> Evaluation
> Teaching relationships and Centers

To get across how teachers might invent as they explore Center teaching, a Center plan has been invented. Questions have been stated with a possible solution to the questions. It is not recommended that the information be used as stated but rather reviewed and adjusted to meet the needs in individual classrooms as the teacher begins to implement Centers.

Proposal Statement

The purpose of this proposal is to describe an organizational arrangement which assists the teacher in:

> changing from a self-contained classroom plan to a team teaching program design

> using Learning Centers as the primary strategy for teaching/learning.

Long Range Purpose

Centers will be designed to serve as a stepping stone to an eventual policy of non-gradedness for instructional tasks

Anticipated Problems and Solutions

THE MOST FREQUENTLY ASKED QUESTIONS? ? ? ?

Problem: How can team members have planning periods together?

Solution: Plan for the students of the three teachers to visit the different specialists during the same block of time.

	M	T	W	Th	Fr
Voight	Libr.	PE	Music		PE
Eden	PE	Libr.	Art		PE
Allen	Art	Music	PE		

Problem: How can teachers arrange classroom space?

Solution: Read pages 35-42

Problem: What new vocabulary will a Center teacher have to use?

Solution: To better understand what is meant by L. C. method the following terms need to be explored. For now, a term will be stated with a brief explanation as to what each means in relation to Center teaching:

Learning Center Method:

> a classroom organizational pattern that serves as an instructional agent so that the teacher and/or student are able to adjust educational tasks to meet individual needs

Learning Center Method/Media:

> a place where media (all forms) are housed for distribution to teachers as learning is individualized
>
> a library area that has been reorganized to include instructional media which allows for independent study activities
>
> a mobile traveling van with educational media that is on loan to a school for a given period of time

Learning Center (in a classroom):

> an instructional display area whereby educational tasks are organized so as to offer for the learner a structured focal point of operation as he sets out to accomplish a learning act

Station for learning or learning station:

> (same as Learning Center)

Display Area:

> a section of the room set aside for student instructional acts to be organized within. This section becomes an instructional agent or lesson designer to provide personalized learning experiences
>
> space for materials, study guides or a specific creation which serves to expose an individual to a topic which might arouse his interest or investment

Learning Center, absorption:

> reading matter at the Learning Center (part or total) of display in which there are no new or strange words which the student can read with complete absorption in meaning
>
> the act of losing oneself in the opportunity to explore a topic

Applying generalizations:

> a learning act whereby the individual uses previously learned generalizations, concepts and/or facts to explain his unfamiliar environment at that moment

Autonomous learning:

> a learning act whereby the student discovers relatively independently the relationships that exist and accounts for the relationship by formulating reasons or understandings

Decentering learning:
> student growth that is not in keeping with the learnings presented at the Center display area(s) so that individual's growth pattern takes another point of view other than the point of view expressed at a given Center(s)

Differentiated Learning Center assignments:
> Center tasks which can be approached at two or more levels of difficulty

Student evaluation packet:
> a series of student evaluation forms that portray the operational level of the student as he performs educational tasks at a Center or Centers

Student evaluation:
> a set of materials and/or tasks which permits the child's understanding to be observed

Pre-evaluation (student):
> an inventory of assets and liabilities an individual brings to a given Center

Re-cycle evaluation:
> - process of evaluating Centers and taking knowledge learned about Center usage to adjust Learning Center procedures and philosophy
> - to begin a new or related learning task for an individual or total class
> - periodically repeated inventory which can be used to record an individual's progress

Teacher Re-tooling:
> this is a process of evaluating Centers and taking knowledge learned about Center usage to adjust Learning Center operational procedures and philosophy

Center evaluation:
> analysis of the pros and cons of each Center and the making of necessary adjustments to improve learning at a Center.

Problem: Are there different types of Learning Centers?

Solution: In researching the topic Centers, the following classification titles were located:

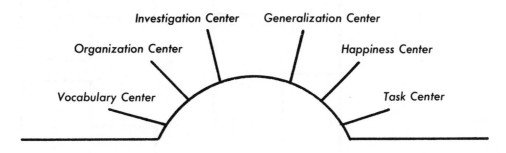

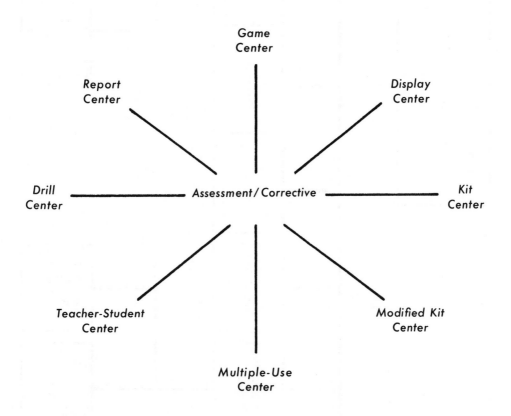

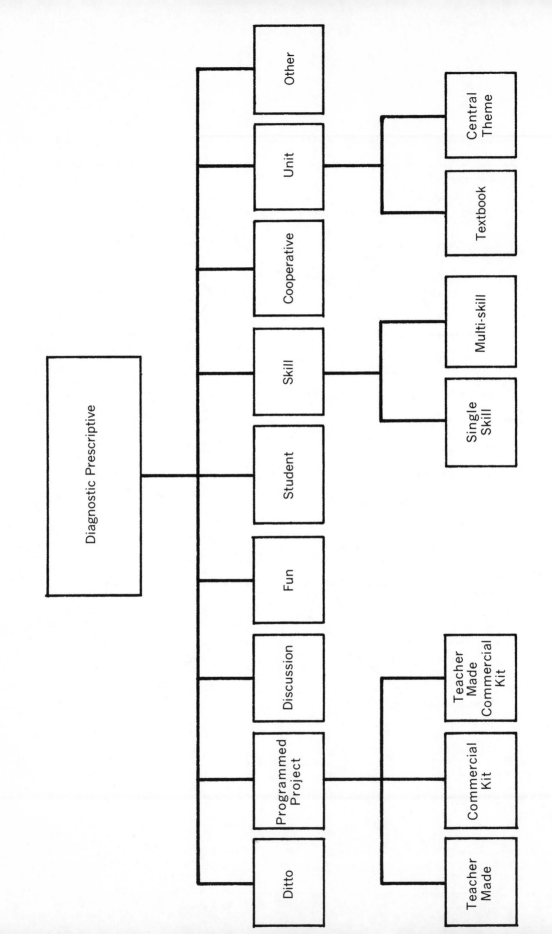

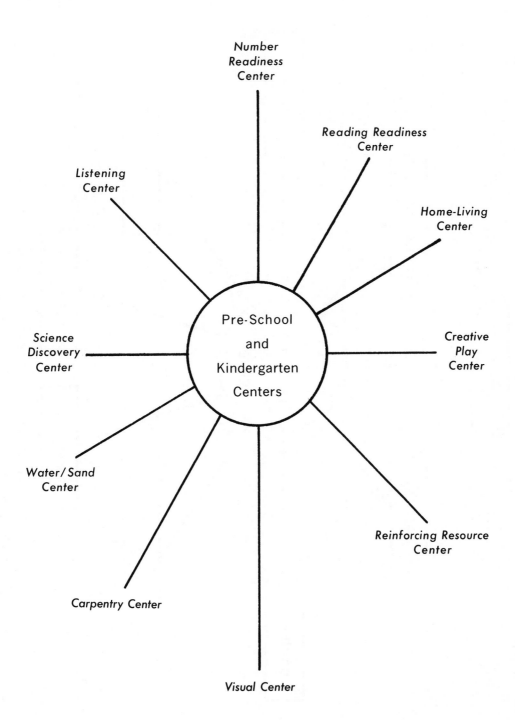

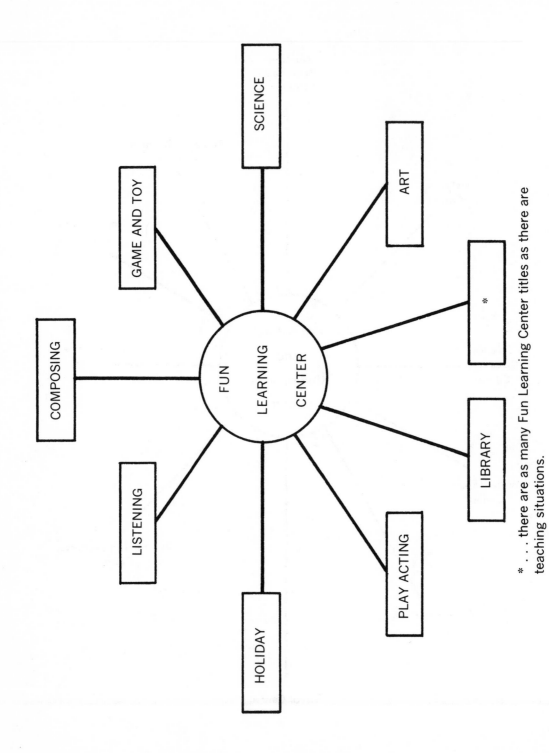

* . . . there are as many Fun Learning Center titles as there are teaching situations.

Problem: How can teachers plan Centers cooperatively in a team setting?

Solution: When centers are planned cooperatively, teachers need to develop communication channels. Each team member must realize what Centers he is responsible for. In order to do this (accept responsibility for designing a given number of Centers) the information might be recorded on forms. Some examples are:

TEAM PLANNING SHEET

Center topic and sub-topics	Team Member Name	Ready Date	Description or comments about Center design

Ecology
  Air pollution
  . . .
Oceanography
  . . .			

PRE-PLANNING WALL CHART

Center Title	Content Area	Ready date and location in room	Skills, concepts, Generalizations	Materials Used	Teacher Comments

RECORD OF CENTERS USED

Language Arts	Social Studies	Mathematics	Science-Health
1. Look Nook	I. The Sea	A.	a.
2.	II.	B.	b.
3.	III.	C.	c.
4.	IV.	D.	d.
5.	V.	E.	e.
6.	VI.	F.	f.
7.	VII.	G.	g.
8.	VIII.	H.	h.
9.	IX.	I.	i.
10.	X.	J.	j.
		. . .	. . .

EQUIPMENT SIGN-OUT FORM

Center Title and Room Location	Equipment Used	Date Out	Date In	Teacher's Name

RATING A CENTER'S WORTH
(Team Members)

```
1  2  3  4  5
Low      High
```

Center Title	Individual Teacher's Rating	Reasons for Score		Team Average

The reasons for a low or high rating would be stated by team members previously during a team planning meeting at the beginning of the school year. This list of reasons for rating a Center would be reviewed often by team members so that the teachers maintain a current criteria for rating Centers.

Problem: What forms can be used to collect data on student progress?

Solution: When the teacher, or team of teachers, want to gather information about student progress, a Student Evaluation Packet needs to be developed. In general, the packet might include the following.

Student Evaluation Packet

Skill/Concept Profile
Progress Goals Checklist
Teacher's Evaluation of Student's Work at a Center
Student Behavior—While at a Center(s)
Evaluation for Week Ending Thursday
Student Teacher Schedule and Assessment
Master Sign-up Form (Group)
Individual Weekly Sign-up Form
Weekly Assessment Sheet
Inventory Assessment Sheet and Prescriptive Task Form
Content Assessment Sheet
    Language Arts
    Social Studies
Pre-conference Sheet
Teacher/Parent Conference Form
Rating Scale of Student Work at Center(s)
Modular Planning Sheet

Note:

These forms have not been arranged in any specific order, nor does the author expect all forms to be used. The ''Center Teacher'' should devise his own evaluation packet to keep to minimum or you'll blow your mind record-shuffling.

SKILL/CONCEPT PROFILE

Name _____   Classroom _____

Conference Comments:

Skill/Concept	Center Title	Center Title	Notation

Notation — Check x in the box to indicate mastery of skill/concept. Notation if not sure of student progress.

PROGRESS GOALS CHECKLIST

Student Name _____

Content Area(s) _____

Progress Goals	No. Times Activity			Comments
	c. 1	c. 2	c. 3	
Arranges ideas in sequence				
Organizes like ideas				
Finds main and major points				
Knows fiction and fact				

The skills which you have included in your objectives and which will become, therefore, the basics for activities at the Centers can be listed on a form in the child's folder.

The Progress Checklist illustrates a technique for reporting student progress to both parents and students. Many commercial companies and "nongraded" schools already have continuous skills listed. From these lists teachers can transfer learning levels onto the above form. This Progress Checklist should only be used when the teacher feels there is a need to portray a level of competence the student has displayed while using a Center or group of Centers. Some teachers have developed a similar Progress Checklist and sent the checklist home in a folder which may also contain report card.

Key:
  C-1   Center One   C-2   Center Two   C-3   Center Three

Number Times Activity
  The teacher checks the number of times a student has attempted to master a progress goal at a particular Center(s) in these columns and makes necessary comments.

TEACHER'S EVALUATION OF STUDENT'S WORK AT A CENTER

Name _____ Classroom _____

Center Title _____ Date _____

Teacher _____

Degree of Effort	Student Attitude	Content Grade	Over-all Rating
Oustanding	Outstanding	A	1
High	High	B	2
Adequate	Adequate	C	3
Acceptable	Acceptable	D	4
Inadequate	Inadequate	E	5

General Comments:

STUDENT BEHAVIOR-WHILE AT A CENTER(S)

Name _____ Classroom _____

Center Title _____ Date _____

Teacher _____

Student Responsibility	Student Interest	Relationship with Adults	Relationship with Students	Over-all Rating
Outstanding	Outstanding	Outstanding	Outstanding	1
Accomplished Easily	High	Accomplished Easily	Accomplished Easily	2
Adequate	Adequate	Adequate	Adequate	3
Acceptable	Acceptable	Acceptable	Acceptable	4
Inadequate	Inadequate	Inadequate	Inadequate	5

General Comments:

EVALUATION FOR WEEK ENDING THURSDAY

Student Name _____

Favorite Center(s) _____

Reasons _____

I learned

Work Habits and/or Work Status

Teacher Eval.	Student Eval.	
		$\sqrt{}$ = Good Habits $\times$ = Need Improvement
☐	☐	Completed daily schedule
☐	☐	Completed various assignments
☐	☐	Moved quickly from Center to Center
☐	☐	Filed work sheets in proper place
☐	☐	Was quiet
☐	☐	Did not disturb others

STUDENT/TEACHER SCHEDULE AND ASSESSMENT

Student Name

Content

Keys: M = Math   PE = Physical Education   Date   Materials Use
       S = Science   . . .   Began   R2² Reading at 2nd grade level
       SS = Social Studies   Completed   (initial of copy will be
                                                                           listed at the front of R)
                                                                           . . .

Date	Center Title	Content Key	Materials Used	Student/Teacher Assessment

MASTER SIGN-UP FORM (GROUP)

Dates and Days	Green Center	Yellow Center	Science Center	Blue Center	Math Center
	ᗩ ᗩ ᗩ ᗩ ᗩ		ᗩ ᗩ ᗩ ᗩ		
			ᗩ ᗩ ᗩ ᗩ ᗩ		
			Closed		
	Closed				

The lines within each block represent how many students may sign up for a Center. If there are no lines then the number of students working at a Center is unlimited.

INDIVIDUAL WEEKLY SIGN-UP FORM

Center Title	Date Began	Work Status	Comments	Completion Date

On the lines under Center Title the student records the Center he is working at.

Work Status Key:
- not completed
- completed

WEEKLY ASSESSMENT SHEET	Math	Science	Social Studies	Reading	Special Interest
Monday					
Tuesday					
Wednesday					
Thursday					
Friday					
End of Week S/T Evaluation					

In place of the content titles shown above, the Center titles can be listed and the student makes the necessary remarks under each title as the need arises.

S/T Student/Teacher

INVENTORY ASSESSMENT SHEET/PRESCRIPTIVE TASK FORM

Student Name _____   Teacher   Date

Date	Center Title	Material Used	Inventory Assessment	Prescriptive Task

CONTENT ASSESSMENT SHEET

(Language Arts)

Name _____   Teacher(s)   Date

Reading

Date	Center	Materials	Student/Teacher Assessment

Oral Expression

Date	Center	Materials	

CONTENT ASSESSMENT SHEET

(Social Studies)

Student Name _____   Teacher's Name   Date

	Date	Center Title	Generalization/Concept	Student/Teacher Assessment
Began				
Completed				
Began				
Completed				

PRE-CONFERENCE SHEET

Student's Name _____

Teacher's Name _____

Content Area and Center Title	Materials Used	Work Status	Student Comments
Social Studies			
World News			
Neighbors to the North			
Science			
Kitchen Science			
Office Science			
Mathematics			
_____			
_____			

Key: Work Status
■ Not Required
√ Completed
3/2 Date Will Complete
○ Not Completed

Note: The same form could be used with the Report Card to explain why a grade was given.

TEACHER/PARENT CONFERENCE FORM

Child's Name _____

Center Areas _____

_____

Date	Center Title	Centers Discussed	Follow-up Recommended

Advantages of this form:
1. Dates appear in order.
2. During the next conference, the teacher can easily follow-up on the "suggestions previously recommended."

RATING SCALE OF STUDENT WORK AT CENTER(S)

Pupil   Classroom   Age   Teacher

Rating Scale

1	2	3	4	5
Low				High

1. How good are work habits?   12345
2. How well can he stick to a task?   12345
3. How well can he follow directions?   12345
4. How well can he complete Center tasks?   12345
5. How well can he select Centers and activities that are appropriate for him?   12345
6. Can he identify the purposes for using a Center?   12345
7. When conferencing how well can he participate in setting goals and objectives?   12345
8. How self-motivated is he in Center planned tasks?   12345
9. Does he become involved in independent activities?   12345
10. Does he become involved in group activities?   12345
11. How well is he able to interact positively with others?   12345
12. How much is he willing to experiment and explore without fear?   12345
13. When a student conferences, is he willing to be accountable for his own actions?   12345
14. Can he work in a manner which does not interrupt or distract others?   12345
15. How well is he able to interact (buddy system) with other pupils in a sharing or helping situation?   12345
16. How is his self-concept as he uses or evaluates Center work?   12345
17. How are his feelings of adequacy in regard to being willing to try new tasks before a teacher conferences with him?   12345

MODULAR PLANNING SHEET

Name

Mon.	Tues.	Wed.	Thurs.	Fri.
I. 9:30-10:30	I. 9:30-10:30	I. 9:30-10:30	I. 9:30-10:30	I. 9:30-10:30
II. 10:30-11:30	II. 10:30-11:30	II. 10:30-11:30	II. 10:30-11:30	II. 10:30-11:30
(Break) III. 11:45-12:40 Lunch	III. 11:45-12:40 Lunch	III. 11:45-12:40 Lunch	(Break) III. 11:45-12:40 Lunch	III. 11:45-12:40 Lunch
IV. 1:40-2:20) Phys. Ed.) 2:50-3:20)	IV. 1:40-2:20) Art) 2:50-3:20)	IV. 1:40-2:20) Phys. Ed.) 2:50-3:20)	IV. 1:40-2:20 Music) 2:50-3:30)	IV. 1:40-2:20) Phys. Ed 2:50-3:20)
Evaluation	Evaluation	Evaluation	Student Evaluation	Evaluation— Teacher/Student

Problem: How can Learning Center teaching be systematized?

Solution: What educators in the past have not tried consistently is to bring order to personalized learning in the classroom when using Learning Centers. Both the administrator and the teacher in the past have been led to believe that the construction of a Center is the "teacher's thing", and/or the Center design is next to impossible to relate to another educator because of the creativity factor.

Center method for personalizing instruction has structure and is easy to implement when the teachers clarify an operational plan of action. Suggested plan as follows:

PLAN OF ACTION

1. Define what Learning Center teaching is (philosophy, organization)
2. Clarify the types of Centers available
3. Establish a format for writing Centers
4. Inventory class needs
5. Design an efficient floor plan
6. Develop an operational style with students

Type of Centers Matched to Student Needs
> Management, schedule
> Records (track of individual school work)
> Conversion techniques
> Material and furniture usage
> Replacing Centers
> Record keeping
> Reporting—students/parents

7. Evaluation of the Total Program
> (Re-cycle evaluation)

Problem: Can a teacher devise a way to improve Center methodology?

Solution: As a teacher uses Centers, he can involve himself in constant evaluation to assist in planned Center Organizational Pattern Change that hopefully leads to Center improvement. This evaluation is called Teacher Retooling and is illustrated below:

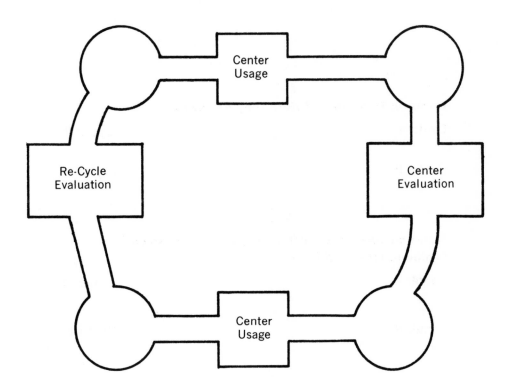

Re-Cycle Evaluation
A process of evaluating Centers and taking knowledge learned about Center usage to adjust Learning Center operational procedures and philosophy.

Center Evaluation
Analyze the pros and cons of each Center and make the necessary adjustments to improve learning at the Center.

To assist the re-tooled teacher in evaluation of Centers, he might want to use an identification sheet to record Center usage information. The following is a model of the identification sheet that a teacher might use:

IDENTIFICATION SHEET

Floor Plan

Notes on Each Center Before They Are Used

Center I   Center III

Center II   Center IV

SECOND PAGE

Notes on Each Center After They Have Been Used
Evaluation (Pro and Con)

Center I   Center III

Center II   Center IV

Rating as to one's value of Center(s)

Key: Low◄——►High

1   5

i.e. Center I —5
Center II —5
Center III—1
Center IV—3

Problem: Will a team have to budget a large amount of money to provide for construction of Centers?

Solution: No, teachers who really want to construct functional Centers do not need a lot of money to purchase special furniture for the classroom. The following classroom model stresses Center areas using existing furniture and cardboard.

TRADITIONAL CLASSROOM MODEL

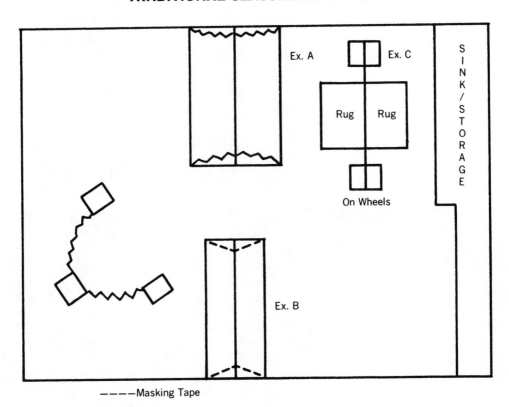

—————Masking Tape

Example A—Desks pushed against cardboard sheets (commercial cardboard or hot water heater boxes) can be used to construct carrells.

Example B—A baby mattress or bottom of TV carton can be placed on top of desks to make a two sided display area. Masking tape over the cardboard and attached to the desk top holds the display area stable. The tape is wrapped around thin wire.

Example C—In place of desks pushed on either side of mattress box, the mattress box can be mounted on a 2 x 4 frame with wheels on the frame so the mattress display area can be pushed aside if the need did arise.

See pages 35-42 in this book.

Problem: What are the different learning styles that Center Method does not compensate for?

Solution: It is possible for most teaching-learning relationships to be classified and used or incorporated into Centers. It should be remembered that most of the teaching-learning relationships can be classified arbitrarily for discussion purposes. Let's assume that the following classification titles represent teaching-learning relationships in the school:

TEACHING-LEARNING RELATIONSHIP TITLES

Lecture	Programmed
Recitation	Demonstration
Project	Group Discussion
Conference	
Games	

To illustrate how the different teaching-learning relationships can be incorporated into Center methodology, the reader must combine Voight's Center classification and teaching-learning relationships cited earlier into a classroom operational pattern for planning.

PATTERN EXAMPLES FOR PLANNING

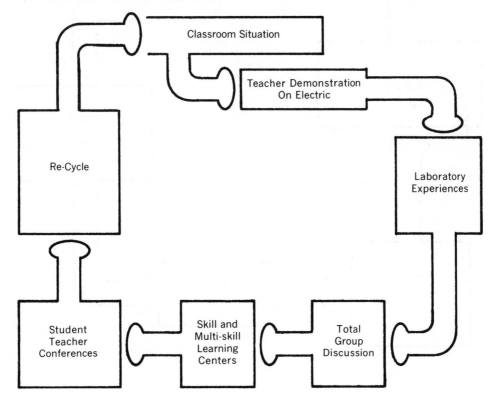

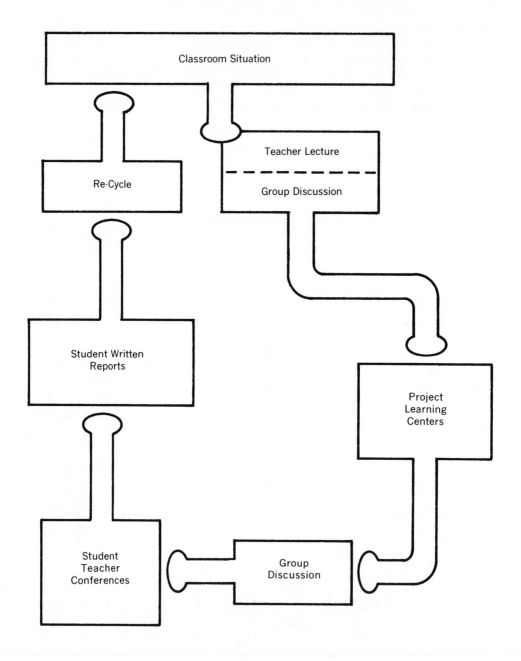

Classroom Situation

Re-Cycle

Teacher Lecture

Group Discussion

Student Written
Reports

Project
Learning
Centers

Student
Teacher
Conferences

Group
Discussion

Another way to visualize how the different teaching-learning relationship can be incorporated into Centers is to design a Center and then list teaching-learning relationships that can be incorporated into the design of a Center.

PATTERN EXAMPLES FOR PLANNING

Display Area

What Floats?

1. Use items on table

2. Record your guess

3. Record your results

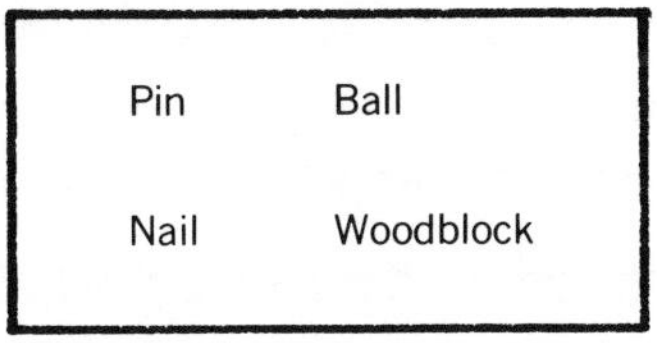

Experience Charts

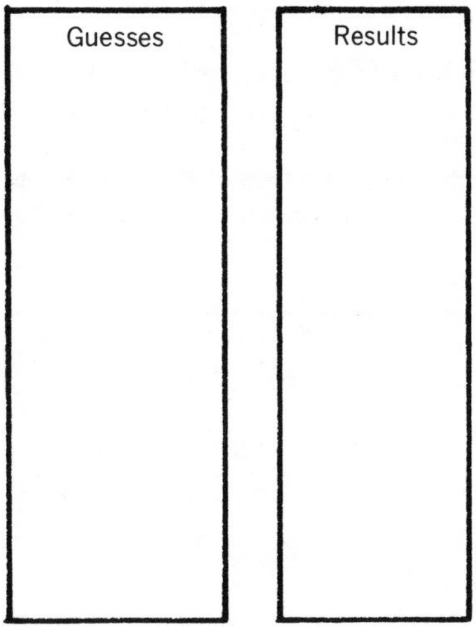

Pin	Ball
Nail	Woodblock

Guesses

Results

TEACHING-LEARNING RELATIONSHIP

Teacher Directed Science Lesson—"Objects that Float"

Student conducts experiments

Group discussion

Related small group experiments

DISPLAY AREA

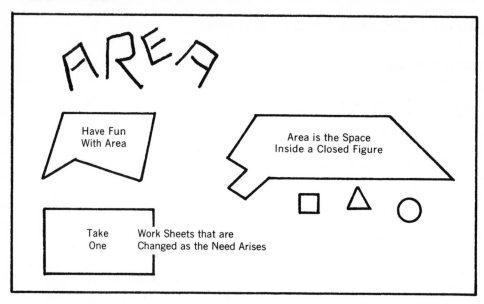

TEACHING-LEARNING RELATIONSHIP

Teacher directed lesson-lecture/group discussion about Area Work Sheets at the Center

Conference with the individual student and during the conference the teacher contracts projects for students to work on

Be The Teacher

Find the grammar mistakes made by Sam Sloppy.

Copy and correct.

Chart Paper
With Incorrect
Grammar Sentences

Completed
Paper

Center Work

Teacher directed textbook lesson

Group discussion of incorrect grammar at the Center

DISPLAY AREA

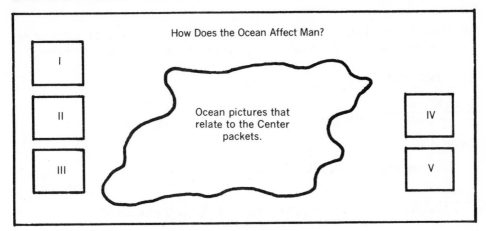

Each packet I-V would contain student work related to the topic OCEAN. The teaching relationship would be an integral part of each packet.

TEACHING-LEARNING RELATIONSHIPS

Packet I   Science Experiments
Packet II   Discussion Questions (Student led)
Packet III Commercial Programmed Materials
Packet IV Teacher Student Conference
Packet V An outgrowth of Packet IV would be a contract for a student to design his own Center on the topic OCEAN-STUDENT LEARNING CENTER.

ANIMAL MOVEMENT

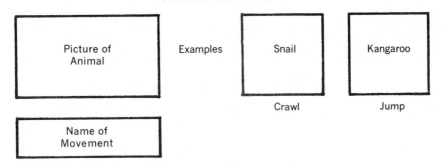

TEACHING-LEARNING RELATIONSHIPS

Group discussion about animal movement and the construction of a Center "Animal Movement."

Film on animals/and add to the Center display pictures and words.

At another Center write experience charts about animals.

Bring in family pets for observation—and record the observation of the animals brought from home.

107

Problem: How can a teacher plan for a range of learning experience at a Center?

Solution: The best way to gain an understanding of a range of learning experience at a Center is to review Centers with learning experience ranges.

ILLUSTRATION I

Educational Task

Provide the child with the experience of computing costs.

Content

Mathematics and Reading

Center Type

Unit (one in a series on money for 6, 7, 8, and 9 year olds)

Center Display

Pictures of items with the price

| piggy bank $1.00 | ball 50c | top 20c |
| kite 88c | rocking horse 75c | |

Work Sheets I	Work Sheets II	Work Sheets III
I	II	III
The top cost_____c	The top cost _____c	The bank cost $_____
The ball cost_____c	The ball cost _____c	The Kite cost _____c
	The total cost is $_____	The dog cost _____c
		The total cost $_____

| (Individual's task is to read and write numbers) | (Individual's task is to read, write and compute with two addends) | (Individual's task is to read, write and compute with three addends) |

POSSIBLE STUDENT FUNCTIONAL LEVELS

A. Do it yourself   B. Ask an aide or buddy   C. Ask teacher
                           for help   for conference

Author's Notes:

The pictures can be either bought cut-outs or models
made during an art project.

LLUSTRATION II

Education Task: To be able to recognize coins (5c, 10c, 25c)

Content: Mathematics and Social Studies

Center Type: Unit Learning Center (one in a series on money for 6, 7,
and 8 year olds).

Display Area: Two display areas A and B. Display area A—Bulletin board
is next to a classroom store.

A

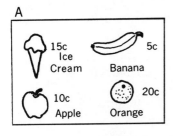

B

Classroom Store

Work Sheets

I-A   How much does each cost?

I-B   How much does each cost?

Orange   _____

Banana   _____

Ice Cream   _____

Apple   _____

II. Go to the classroom store to find the cost and read chart 3.

Lemon _____   Candy Apple _____

Carrots _____   Gum _____

III. Add the cost of these store items:

(a)	(b)	(c)	(d)
Apple _____	Gum _____	 _____	 _____
Banana_____	Candy Apple _____	 _____	 _____
Total _____	Total _____	Total_____	Total_____

B. Store Area Next to Bulletin Board

The store features the following:

_____ Pictures that relate to worksheets about store items

_____ Actual store signs with prices on them

_____ Store items   (Additional Learning

_____ Play cash register   Experience Would Be
                                          Planned)

Author's Notes:	General store area with an aide (older student) directing store activities on making change. The level of difficulty when making change will depend on the needs of the students visiting the Center.

Chart III at the store would be as follows:

Chart III

The orange cost 20c

The ice cream cost 15c   (The chart(s) relate to the

The apple cost 10c   worksheets in Display Area A and B)

ILLUSTRATION III

   Educational Task: To provide an experience so that the student is able
   to use numbers 1-50 when paper money is involved.

   Content: Mathematics

   Center Type: Unit Learning Center (one in a series on money for 6, 7,
   and 8 year olds)

Display Area

Dog $10.00   Cat $5.00

| Picture | | | Picture |

Bulletin Board Model
Constructed by
Teacher

Picture Space for Child to Use

I went to the pet shop.   (Student draws a picture of the pet he wants
                                       to buy. Each student is given his own primary
I went to buy a _____   sheet of paper to complete the task.)

It will cost_____

Author's Notes: The learning experience range can be widened when the teacher
has a conference with the student.
This basic model can be used for the following Center subject
topics: farm, zoo, fish, safety, birds.

ILLUSTRATION IV

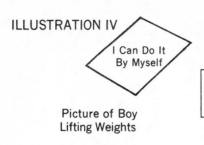

I Can Do It
By Myself

Picture of Boy
Lifting Weights

DICTIONARY SKILLS

1. Take work sheet from the folder.
2. Use your dictionary to help you spell.

1. Sign Up 2. Sheet 3.	Worksheet I	Worksheet II	Completed Sheets

WORKSHEET I

Direction: Roll the die and see if you can spell a word from the beginning sound that might fit into the following sentences:
1. (The teacher must first locate the
2. die that has the beginning sounds
3. she wants the students to practice
4. and then construct worksheets to fit
   the needs of the students.)

WORKSHEET II

a. Write three sentences using the pronouns he, she, and it.
b. Substitute pronouns for the nouns in the following sentences:
1. John rode home in a car.
2. Where is Mary?
3. Can you find the book?

ILLUSTRATION V

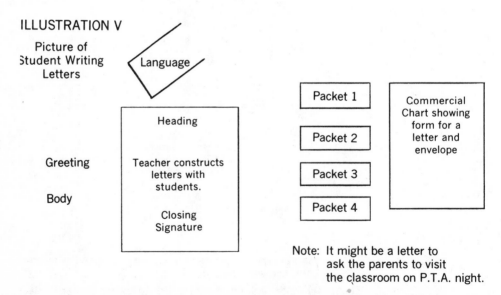

Picture of
Student Writing
Letters

Language

Greeting

Body

Heading

Teacher constructs
letters with
students.

Closing
Signature

Packet 1

Packet 2

Packet 3

Packet 4

Commercial
Chart showing
form for a
letter and
envelope

Note: It might be a letter to
ask the parents to visit
the classroom on P.T.A. night.

Each packet represents a different level of learning. For this Center many of the commercial dittos can be used.

The pictures of students writing letters in the Center display area could be actual pictures of students in the classroom writing letters or large cut-out pictures of children writing.

ILLUSTRATION VI

TOPIC—The Family

TYPE—Cooperative Learning Center

PURPOSE—To familiarize the child with the different home conditions in our community.

DISPLAY AREA—

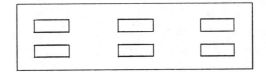

MATERIALS—Snapshots of family life
        Flannel board
        Commercial kits on family living
        Chart paper

TEACHING-LEARNING RELATIONSHIP
    Teacher demonstration with visual aids
    Student group discussion sessions
    Student reports—the student brings in snapshots to be placed on the bulletin board while they respond about their family life
    Family role-playing experiences

ILLUSTRATION VII

TOPIC—School Family

TYPE—Unit Learning Center

PURPOSE—To identify the duties of the school resource personnel

DISPLAY AREA—

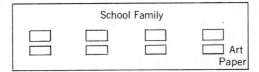

MATERIALS — Snapshots of personnel (Principal, secretary, librarian, custodian, bus driver, cafeteria manager)
    Bulletin board
    Name tags and titles of personnel
    Tape recorder and earphone
    Art paper
    Crayons

CENTER ACTIVITY— Children listen to tape where each school family member states their important duties in relation to the children in the classroom and the total school environment. The child draws an activity of one member of the school family.

EVALUATION—During the child/teacher conference, the teacher will write a sentence, dictated by the pupil, to describe the activities of a school member(s).

Problem: After group experiences have been planned, does the teacher need to be aware of any special management techniques?

Solution: Some suggestions:

a. Discuss student learning assignments at Centers, with the whole class before students go to work and infer at which Centers students can work together.

b. Stop from time to time to conference with students who have common problems and make group experience assignments based on the outcome.

c. On a chart, list group experiences that students have a choice of doing.

d. Plan total group programs (culminating activities) that require group interaction.

e. Assume school-wide responsibilities and organize as a group project.

Problem: How can teachers train students to use Centers?

Solution: To train students to use the Centers is not possible but to involve them in specific classroom experiences allows the student to understand the operational pattern behind Center Methodology. Basically the student needs to be able to handle himself in:

> reading directions
> using AV equipment
> conferencing with the teacher
> planning learning experiences
>   independently or cooperatively
>   with the teacher or peer members

Author's Notes
This list is not complete and expands as the needs arise.

114

Problem: How can volunteer aides be used?

Solution: During the Center usage volunters might be used to:
Keep records
Passout and collect pupil materials
Read a story to a group of pupils
Work with pupils as they use programmed materials
Assist pupils in understanding directions (oral or written)
Read materials that a pupil finds too difficult
  Complete assignment with pupil
Assist in moving pupils from one activity to another
Play educational games with pupils
Tutor pupils on a regular basis
Visit the library to help pupils select books
Type pupils' creative stories
Gather information about work habits of pupils
Use AV equipment with pupils
Develop bulletin board displays with pupils
Introduce a Center

. . .

Problem: Should the community be informed about changing to Center teaching?

Solution: Yes, however, a general meeting to inform the community is not the only method of communicating the change. Groundwork that leads up to a general meeting can follow many avenues for communicating to the community in general.

For discussion, let's assume the teacher(s) has decided to gradually move into using Centers. Then he might want to implement the following ideas:

(a) Form a PTA Committee to visit neighboring schools that claim they have an innovative instructional program—programmed material to Learning Centers.
(b) Invite parents to be aides in the school so they can view Centers in operation.
(c) Encourage interschool visitation whereby the students, parents, and teachers visit other schools to view a school that uses Learning Centers.
(d) Plan informal small group conferences for parents.
(e) Develop a teacher or team handbook to explain Center usage. The categories for the handbook might include the following:
Center definition
Classification Chart with models of Learning Centers for each type
Evaluation techniques
Pictures of Centers
(f) . . .

Problem: Can materials be purchased that are designed for Center usage?

Solution: Almost any and/all insturctional materials can be adapted. If the question refers to specific Canned Programs, I am happy to answer, "No Canned Program is on the market, yet."

Dr. John Nickols and Ralph Voight have attempted to offer basic ways teachers can organize so as to use commercial and teacher-made instructional materials. For an idea of materials that are available, review the following:

COGNITIVE SYSTEMS LCL STARTER PACKAGE

Cognitive Measurements: The developmental Activity Investigation Techniques, or AITd Tasks, have special value in revealing various levels of cognitive functioning at a given time. AITd Tasks are easily administered to second graders and older children at the Inventory Center. They are scored by the classroom teacher and provide her with three types of scores. A special table is provided so that each score can be converted to a dQ which ranges from 10 to 160. A dQ of 60s indicates minimal expectancy for Second Graders; 70F for Fourth Graders; 80S for Sixth Graders. Minimal expectancy points to the expected score for a given age or grade level. Any lesser score for a given age or grade placement would suggest a crucial need for special developmental exercises in the functions which are being measured by a specific test. A score which exceeds minimal expectancy can show "average" or "advanced" cognitive functioning, but it is not capable of indicating the actual IQ of any one student. There are 35 AITd Booklets in the starter packet.

Look at the *PTd Score* to indicate additional work at the Prescriptive Center. Tasks might be assigned in analogous reasoning, inductive reasoning, abstract comparisons, and other aspects of Problem-Solving when non-verbal materials are used. Younger children can use discovery approaches in building things or in playing visual games. Sample items are provided in the NL1s and NL1 Booklets to be discussed.

Reflection Exercises: Booklets NL1s and NL1 were designed specifically for such uses as those which might be made at the Prescriptive Center. No scoring is done. The child may offer any explanation for his performances. The goal is to require him to "think through" each response. Use thin copy paper for repeated use of each booklet. NL1s is used first. Pages 1 and 2 contain paper-and-pencil exercises. The teacher can make additional tasks on 3 by 5 cards for children who will need additional exercises of the types contained on these pages. Page 3 requires the use of blocks. These may be either (a) triangular, square or rectangular blocks, or (b) cubes which have solid colors on four sides and two colors on the remaining two sides (purchased at a toy mart for $5.00 or less). Page 4 requires the use of stick numbers. Purchase these at a toy mart (for about $2.00) and paint a number of the lengths from units to 10's. Just two colors are necessary for two or three of each length. NL1 is used last. For pages 3 and 4, it is necessary to purchase plastic tile and pegboard or wooden blocks similar to those used for page 3 of the NL1s Booklet (usually for $3.00 or less at a toy mart).

Imaginative Exercises: One focus for imaginative exercises at the Fun Center is the book *Corpie. Corpie* was written to facilitate the process of reading, but also to permit group interaction activities. It has special merit in facilitating integrated arts activities. It permits expressive reading, interpretative role-playing, and audience participation. Children can make masks of both the expressive and aesthetic forms, in order to adapt the material for a play. Special props can be made. Special sound effects can be devised . . .

A Product With a Purpose Publication, HSD, 1970
HSD Branch Office, 2220 Reddfield Drive, Falls Church, Va. 22043

LC TEACHER GUIDE
JOHN NICKOLS AND RALPH VOIGHT

Student Names	Note	LQ	dQ	Cognitive Measurements IP	VL	PT	PI	NLi Need	Circle One for Extra LC Work	Planning Information
1.								1 2 3 4	(SD Co Pr Fun)	
2.								1 2 3 4	(SD Co Pr Fun)	
3.								1 2 3 4	(SD Co Pr Fun)	
4.								1 2 3 4	(SD Co Pr Fun)	
5.								1 2 3 4	(SD Co Pr Fun)	
6.								1 2 3 4	(SD Co Pr Fun)	
7.								1 2 3 4	(SD Co Pr Fun)	
8.								1 2 3 4	(SD Co Pr Fun)	
9.								1 2 3 4	(SD Co Pr Fun)	
10.								1 2 3 4	(SD Co Pr Fun)	
11.								1 2 3 4	(SD Co Pr Fun)	
12.								1 2 3 4	(SD Co Pr Fun)	
13.								1 2 3 4	(SD Co Pr Fun)	
14.								1 2 3 4	(SD Co Pr Fun)	
15.								1 2 3 4	(SD Co Pr Fun)	
16.								1 2 3 4	(SD Co Pr Fun)	
17.								1 2 3 4	(SD Co Pr Fun)	
18.								1 2 3 4	(SD Co Pr Fun)	
19.								1 2 3 4	(SD Co Pr Fun)	
20.								1 2 3 4	(SD Co Pr Fun)	
21.								1 2 3 4	(SD Co Pr Fun)	
22.								1 2 3 4	(SD Co Pr Fun)	
23.								1 2 3 4	(SD Co Pr Fun)	
24.								1 2 3 4	(SD Co Pr Fun)	
25.								1 2 3 4	(SD Co Pr Fun)	
26.								1 2 3 4	(SD Co Pr Fun)	
27.								1 2 3 4	(SD Co Pr Fun)	
28.								1 2 3 4	(SD Co Pr Fun)	
29.								1 2 3 4	(SD Co Pr Fun)	
30.								1 2 3 4	(SD Co Pr Fun)	
31.								1 2 3 4	(SD Co Pr Fun)	
32.								1 2 3 4	(SD Co Pr Fun)	
33.								1 2 3 4	(SD Co Pr Fun)	
34.								1 2 3 4	(SD Co Pr Fun)	
35.								1 2 3 4	(SD Co Pr Fun)	

Punch appropriate holes and place guide sheets in a notebook as these become available. The Following check list is to help the teacher prepare a Learning Center Classroom.

_____ 1 Read the LC Book, *Learning Center,* by Ralph C. Voight.

_____ 2 Read the leaflet entitled *LC Abstract.*

_____ 3 Read the leaflet, *Cognitive System Learning Center Laboratory.*

_____ 4 Read the leaflet, *Cognitive System LCL Starter Package.*

_____ 5 Organize the Learning Centers you select: structure your room.

_____ 6 Place materials on hand about the classroom easily accessible to students while working at each respective Learning Center to be in use.

_____ 7 Plan a place for each student's personal belongings and other essentials.

_____ 8 Plan a temporary set for each child, plus initial activities for several days, pending further observations and definite starting activities.

_____ 9 Fill in the class roll (in spaces provided above). Use the ''note'' space for necessary data, such as sex, age, grade, IQ, achievement score, etc., which is available and might be of value for planning initial activities.

_____10 Initial activities should permit observations on each child's academic skills, learning needs (*e.g.,* carrel-like seats for distractibility or help for dependent children), and social needs (*e.g.,* fun-activities for shyness).

_____11 Use four to six carrel-like seats to begin the inventory activities. Read the leaflet *Cognitive Measurements with the AITd and NLi Booklets,* plus three Booklets, *The AIT System, Administering AITc Tasks* and *Scoring AITc Responses.*

_____12 Administer AITd Tasks (one test booklet), score the responses and record the results in the column marked dQ, IP, VL and PT. If the AITc Tasks are available (in a total of three test booklets), administer and score these and record the results in the columns marked LQ, dQ, IP, VL, PT and PI.

_____13 Inspect AIT columns and circle the developmental LC at which extra work is prescribed on the basis of the cognitive measurements. Circle the Skill Development (SD) Notation for the 20% of the students with the lowest IP Ranks. The Cooperative (Co) LC is circled for low VL Ranks; Prescriptive (Pr) LC for low PT Ranks. If PI Ranks are listed, the Fun LC might be appropriate.

_____14 Notice the LQ (when four Ranks are used) or dQ (when IP, VL and PT Ranks are used), and compare these with expectancy for your class. Expectancy for LQ is 40k for Grade K, 50f for 1 and 60s for 2. LQ or dQ expectancy is 65 for 3, 70F for 4, 75 for 5, 80S for 6, 85 for 7, and 90I for 8 or above. If LQ or dQ is below expectancy, the IP, VL, PT and/or PI Ranks which accounts for it could suggest a need for even additional developmental work.

_____15 Administer the introductory New Learning Exercises, or Booklet NLi, and circle the page number, 1, 2, 3 and/or 4, for any difficulties which are observed. Page 1 of the NLi Booklet lists appropriate exercises.

_____16 Read leaflet *Developmental LC's,* study booklets NL1s, NL1, NL2s, and NL2, and design operative Prescription, Skill Development and Cooperative LC's to include developmental exercises. Also read the booklet *Scoring AITc Responses* again.

_____17 Read the leaflet *The Fun Center* and design a Fun LC.

_____18 Read the leaflet *LC Abstract* and design Academic LC's.

_____19 Plan an appropriate range of activities for your class at the Inventory, each Development and each Academic LC.

_____20 Be ready to work with local and outside Consultants to design and maintain optimal LC's and make full use of these.

Use the space below to write in additional check items.

Problem: How might the school become involved in using Centers?

Solution: Two examples of how the school might become involved are ATLUOP (Administrator-Teacher—Learning Unit Organizational Pattern) and College Course.

Example I—ATLUOP

When beginning to implement Centers, the staff might want to participate in a total school problem-theme unit—ATLUOP.

ATLUOP—Administrator-Teacher-Learner Unit
Organization Pattern

ATLUOP is an organizational procedure that can be used to implement Center usage. The following comments about ATLUOP are stated for the purpose of offering a way a total faculty could move into Center usage:

ATLUOP

Realizing that educators are constantly concerned with what content and experiences are taught at the grade level below or above, a school organizational pattern needs to be designd so as to allow an atmosphere for the administrator, teacher, and learner to communicate effectively on student content experiences.

Due to hardware, teaching materials, libraries, and extensive classroom planning to personalize learning, our schools have taken steps forward. Many times news programs are designed for the whole school. However, the developmental phases of personalized learning are not really communicative by all school participants K-6.

The putting together of a K-6 developmental phases of learning is not visible to school participants because they rarely have an occassion to communicate to each other outside of a worshop, to explain said program or to review a chart in front of the teacher's edition of the materials being used.

If there is one term that should be used more in education to specify that instruction has related developmental phases the tacher and learner must be aware of when planning curriculum usage in the elementary school, it is ATLUOP. . . .

In this situation, ATLUOP is the pulling together of content and learning experiences at the total school level so that teachers and learners develop instructional acts that are interrelated with learnings, rather than participants experiencing K or 6th unrelated instructional acts. Too often a third grade teacher and learner plan individualized learning without being aware of the experience acts taken by participants at another grade level or below.

In order to overcome fragmented instructional acts in the elementary school, the total school organizational pattern has to be so designed that teachers and learners involve themselves in planning sequential acts (experiences) for children.

For each school ATLUOP planning and usage will be defined operationally differently. The general model will be basically the same.

SELECTION MODEL PROCESS

Selection of Total School Problem Theme and Culmination Activity(s)

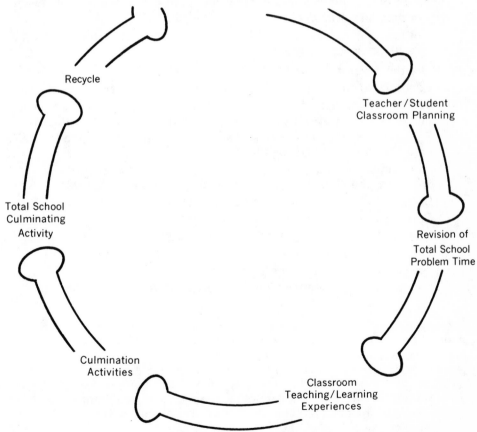

Recycle

Teacher/Student
Classroom Planning

Total School
Culminating
Activity

Revision of
Total School
Problem Time

Culmination
Activities

Classroom
Teaching/Learning
Experiences

How is the school-wide problem theme selected?

Faculty members select a high interest topic with a school-wide problem theme that individual teachers can return to the classroom and plan student experiences. Some high interest areas, K-6 grades, that have been used by educators are:

Interest Area	School-wide Problem Theme
Money	The staff develops a total
Space	school problem theme and each
Pollution	teacher then constructs sub-themes
Oceanography	with the students to plan learning
Five Senses	experiences around.

When selecting an ATLUOP problem theme, staff members might ask these questions:

Are the content and educational acts suited to the maturation of the students and to the physical and psychological needs of the students?

Do the school plans provide for articulation at the total school level?

Are materials available?

Is it possible to provide for flexibility so that students and teachers are able to plan cooperatively?

What are the advantages and/or characteristics of ATULOP?

Coordinated curriculum learnings K-6 at the school level.

Familiarize the teachers on the staff with learning acts (experiences) students are exposed to whether they be K or 6th grade students.

Students over the years develop a learning base from which future experiences are built or expanded

An organizational pattern that reveals what developmental phases (outline form) are being taught to specific age children or grades.

Content and learning acts are planned with a wholeness vision

Cuts across subject lines—interrelatedness of content

Learning is based upon personal needs of students' drives and desires

Cooperative planning at all levels—administrative, teacher, learner

Democratic planning is implemented

Emphasis on problem-solving as it relates to the world of the child

. . .

The advantages of such a program are many more than what has been outlined above. The steps that one has to perform to carry forth ATLUOP are not complex nor do they require educators to develop complex plans. Meetings—(convert a few of the dull faculty meetings into short fact-finding sessions and the ATLUOP planning will have been completed) are needed as a vehicle for developing dialogue patterns so that teachers can communicate educational teaching acts they are using with students in the individual classroom. (See figure I on next page.)

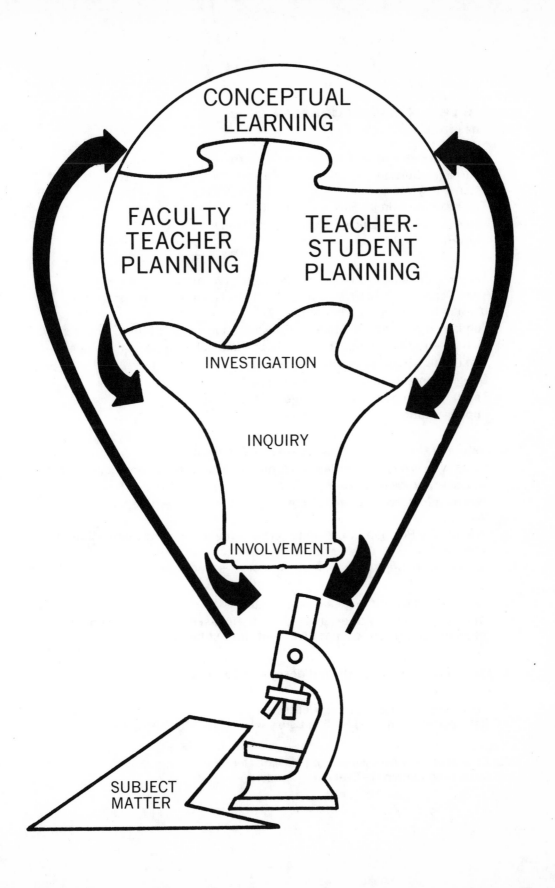

EXAMPLE II—COLLEGE COURSE
Outline of Topics

A. Curriculum as a Basic Educational Concern
   Source for Curriculum Concern: reasons for concern, parent, student, teacher involvement
   The need for a Broad Field Curriculum
   Professional Dominance in Curriculum Planning
   Pattern of Organization

B. Learning Centers as an Instructional Agent for Instructing Students
   The Problems Behind Learning Center Usage — Learning Centers as method for organizing instruction
   Fundamental Teacher/Student Consideration when Centers are Implemented—traditional influences—role of the teacher—role of the student—role of the parent, authority, responsibilities
   Design Elements that make up a Center
   Teach re-tooling for Center usage
   Implementation

C. Nature of the Learning Process when using Centers
   Kinds of Learning: motor learning, mental association, conditioning, trial and error, problem solving . . .
   Teaching Methods: lecture, discussion, conferences, programmed instruction . . .
   Individual's Position in Learning: growth, development, maturation, environment
   Forces which affect/effect Learning: home, school, society

D. Defining and Classifying Learning Centers
   Types with examples of each: single and mutli-skill, project, programmed, programmed-project, cooperative, unit, fun, student . . .

E. Identifying student needs and designing Centers

F. Objectives and the Learning Center
   Before using Center(s)—While using Center(s)—After using Center(s)

G. Evaluation and Assessment of Learning Centers
   Evaluating Center(s)—Evaluating Student(s)

SESSIONS

1. The Challenges of Teaching in the Elementary School
2. Explore the Methods of Teaching, and Relate These Methods to Individualizing Instruction in the Classroom
3. Study the Learning Theories That Support Center Teaching
4. Cite Examples of How Learning Centers Complement the Theories Behind Child Development
5. Curriculum Organization and Planning When Centers are Used in a School
6. Balancing the Areas of Instruction as Centers are Implemented and Used
7. Language Arts   Foreign Language   Social Studies
8. Physical Education
9. Mid-term Examination
10. Review Mid-term and Select Project Reports
11. Classify and Define the Different Types of Centers Available to the Classroom Teacher
12. Write a Traditional Unit and Compare Learning Center Teaching to Unit Teaching
13. Objective Writing When Planning or Evaluating Instruction-Learning Centers
14. Evaluation of Center Method
    a. Parent Evaluation of the Program
    b. Student Evaluation as He Uses Centers
    c. Teacher Evaluation as Centers are Used (Pre-Evaluation andRecycle Evaluation)
15. Summary Session to Prepare for the Final Examination
16. Final Examination

REQUIREMENTS

- 3 short quizzes (25 minutes each)
- mid-term examination
- oral report on topics selected by the professor as course develops
- term paper
- final examination

Problem: How can Centers assist the student who has emotional psychoedu-cational difficulties?

Solution: The psychologist on the staff will be invited to attend meetings and assist in designing specific Centers. A review written by John Nickols repro-duced below indicates the direction the team plans to take as they design specific Centers for children with learning disabilities:

"REVIEW"

. . . The Learning Center approach could be viewed as one of the most prom-ising innovations of our time for the practicing clinical psychologist. This is certainly true of Ralph Voight's contribution.

Essentially, Mr. Voight conceptualizes three basic types of Learning Centers which might operate in a complementary manner to facilitate well-rounded de-velopment of the total child. His Inventory Learning Center permits cur-rent data from repeated evaluation to be recycled back through the process of classroom planning and team teaching in order to serve the current needs of the individual child. He allows for the establishment of Developmental Learning Centers in his Cooperative, Prescriptive, Skill Development, and Fun Learning Centers, any one of which might be modified to provide the oppor-tunity for basic cognitive processes and social skills to be exercised. His Aca-demic Learning Centers are well exemplified in the Unit, Student, Project, and Programmed Centers which promote educational achievement.

The advantage of Voight's contribution is that some of the information which is obtained during the interaction between the psychologist and the child can also be recycled via parental consent through the ongoing process of class-room planning and team teaching. Since Voight's Learning Center approach is already child-centered, provision is already established for incorporating suggestions from the clinician into the plans for working with the individual child.

A knowledge of the purpose of each type of Learning Center will permit the clinician to inform himself of both the types of Learning Centers which are in use in a given classroom and the day-to-day observations by the teacher in order to orient some suggestions towards effective classroom usage. . . .

. . . The practicing clinical psychologist who works with emotional or psycho-educational difficulties in children should inform himself about this approach so that he can direct suggestions which might be used by a teacher or teach-ing team in planning the individual's work at some of the Key Learning Cen-ters. The Skill Development, Cooperative, Prescriptive, and Fun Learning Cen-ters should be given special consideration.

Problem: Should all classrooms have Centers in them?

Solution: That is impossible to answer, but general plans can be outlined and implemented as the need arises. Some general plans are:

EXAMPLE I—DEPARTMENTAL PLAN
Each teacher has a classroom and a content area assigned to him. In general, a typical classroom might resemble the following design:

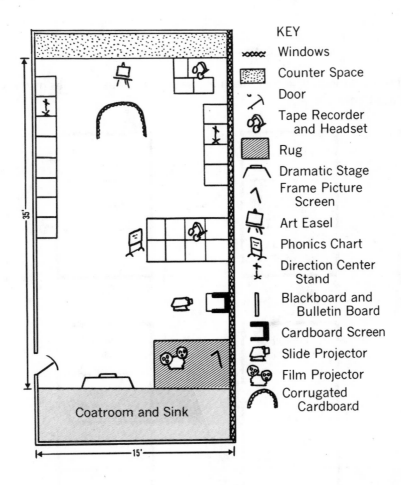

KEY

xxxxx	Windows
	Counter Space
	Door
	Tape Recorder and Headset
	Rug
	Dramatic Stage
	Frame Picture Screen
	Art Easel
	Phonics Chart
	Direction Center Stand
	Blackboard and Bulletin Board
	Cardboard Screen
	Slide Projector
	Film Projector
	Corrugated Cardboard

EXAMPLE II—COMMONS PLAN

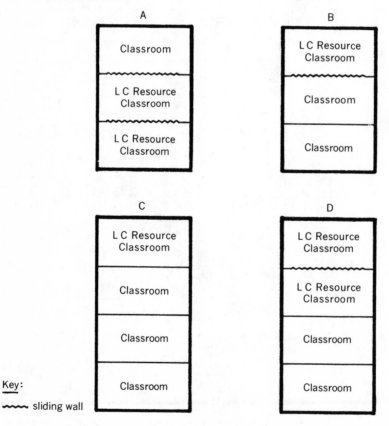

Two Classrooms

Library

COMMONS WORK AREA

Students work in this area in Centers while (2) teachers are in classrooms with small groups of students. The Learning Centers are manned by a teacher and an aide.

Administrative Office

EXAMPLE IV—RESOURCE ROOM PLAN

The teachers might plan together and use a classroom or series of classrooms to house Centers in—

A

Classroom

L C Resource Classroom

L C Resource Classroom

B

L C Resource Classroom

Classroom

Classroom

C

L C Resource Classroom

Classroom

Classroom

Classroom

D

L C Resource Classroom

L C Resource Classroom

Classroom

Classroom

Key:

〜〜 sliding wall

EXAMPLE III—ACTIVITY ORIENTATED PLAN

The major feature of the plan is that the teachers have the activities classified as to the number of people participating in an activity. In general, Room A would have large group activities, Room B would have small group to semi-independent activities, and Room C would have independent activities.

A.

B.

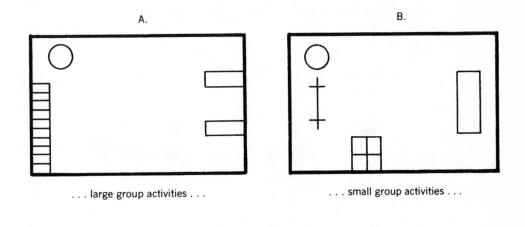

. . . large group activities . . .

. . . small group activities . . .

C.

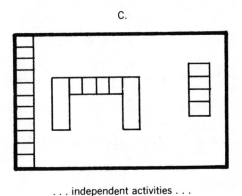

. . . independent activities . . .

Problem: Can examples be cited of Centers teachers have used?

Solution: Some examples are:

Permission granted by authors for use by: Ann Shade, Pam Gray, Sunta Rosappe, Sandy Zimmerman, Anna E. Weedy, Elizabeth Melone, Patricia Brown.

UNIT LEARNING CENTER

Objective: To compare Indian cultures and to understand the variations of life patterns in different parts of the world.

Center #1:

    Topic: Motivation

    Type of Center: Observation Center

    Objective: To awaken interest in Indian cultures.

    Materials:

        Display an area with Indian artifacts, trade books, magazine articles, pamphlets, etc.

    Display:

    Student Directions: Join the Pow Wow!

                    Look and Read.

    Evaluation: Teacher observes children's interest in the Center.

Center #2:

    Topic: Social Studies Unit

    Type of Center: Programmed Learning Center

    Objective: To acquaint the children with Indian culture.

    Materials:

        Programmed materials—text and records

        Record player

        Earphones

Display:

Student Directions:
1. Sit down.
2. Put on earphones.
3. Turn to page
4. Put on record #
5. Now look and listen.

Evaluation:
1. Teacher/class discussion of material covered at the Center.
2. Teacher/student conference in which student retells the story using the pictures in the text.

Center #3:
Topic: Research
Type of Center: Multi-Skill Learning Center
Objective: To teach research skills at level of class
Materials:
Encyclopedia
Trade books
Social Studies texts
Magazines
Pamphlets
Paper
Pencils

Display:

*Topics can be changed according to children's interest.

Student directions:
1. Choose a topic.
2. Read about the topic.
3. Write a short story.
4. Draw a picture for your story.
5. Put your work in the right pocket.

Evaluation:

Teacher/group evaluation in which each child reads and discusses his research story. The teacher might make an outline for these four topics if she feels the group is ready for beginning outline skills.

Center #4:

Topic: Spelling

Type of Center: Single Skill

Objective: To develop a list of words which a child can use in creative writing and research activities.

Materials:

Cloud-shaped papers

Pencils

Child's own word list from research, creative writing, etc.

Social Studies texts

Trade books

Magazines

Pamphlets

Display:

Side 1   Side 2

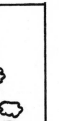

Name	Name	Name	Name

Student Directions:
1. Make a list of ten Indian words you would like to know.
2. Write each word on a cloud.
3. Pin your cloud on the board.
4. Learn to spell your word.

Evaluation:
Teacher/class period in which a student can present known words to the class. Words are then entered under the student's name on Side 2 of the Center.

Center #5:
Topic: Audio-Visual Center
Type of Center: Multi-Skill Center
Objective: To increase the student's knowledge of Indian cultures.
Materials:
Record player—earphones
Record—filmstrip—book sets
Filmstrip projector

Display:

Look and Listen

Student Directions:

    Look and listen

Evaluation:

    None

Center #6:

    Topic: Creative Activities

    Type of Center: Fun Center

    Objective: To provide an area in which the children have an opportunity
        to express creatively the knowledge from their research on the unit.

    Materials:

        All types of art materials

        Records (Indian dances)

        Record player

        Earphones

        Tape recorder

    Display:

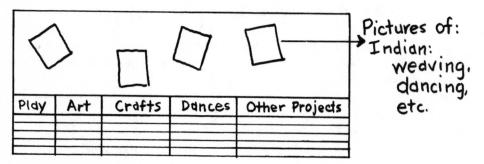

Student Directions:

    1. Write your name under a topic.

    2. Indian Fun Day will be _____ .

Evaluation:

    Participation in the class program, Indian Fun Day.

              *   *   *

Notes:

    1. Centers #2 and #4 are required.

    2. Culminating evaluation:

        a. Indian Fun Day in which class participates.

        b. Pencil and paper test with questions taken from Centers #2
           and #4. Children can contribute questions to the test.

Topic: Final consonants

Type of Center: Single Skill

Objective: To provide further practice in identifying final consonants.

Materials: Four sets of tagboard cards. Each card containing a picture with the word written under it, omitting the final consonant. Paper and pencils.

Example:

Display area:

Student Directions:
1. Take a set of cards.
2. Look at each picture.
3. Say each word.
4. Listen for the final sound.
5. Write each word with its final sound.

Evaluation: Given a list of words stated orally by the teacher at a pupil conference, student names or writes the letter that stands for the final consonant sound of each word. A worksheet to hand in may be left at the station.

Topic: Sequence

Type of Center: Single Skill

Objective: To recall events of familiar stories and place these events in sequence.

Materials: Assorted SeeQuees

Display Area:

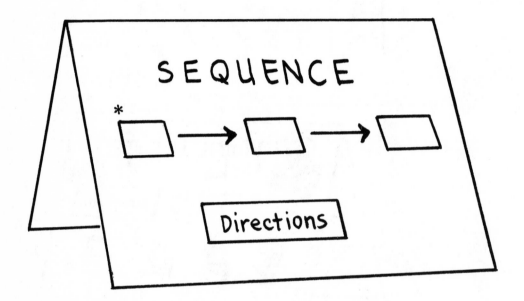

Student Directions:

1. Take a board.
2. Look at the pictures.
3. Think about the story.
4. Put the pictures in order.
5. Call the teacher when you are finished.

Evaluation:

Teacher/student conference in which student retells the story using the pictures.

*Three-picture sequence

Topic: Initial consonants

Type of Center: Single Skill

Objectives: To provide further practice in identifying initial consonants.

Materials: Three sets of tagboard cards. Each card has a picture with the word written under it, omitting the initial consonant.

Example:

Answer sheet for each set of cards.   Paper.

Display Area:

Student Directions:
1. Take a set of cards.
2. Look at each picture.
3. Say each word.
4. Listen for the beginning sound.
5. Write each word with its beginning sound.

Evaluation:
Given a list of words stated orally by the teacher at a pupil conference, student names or writes the letter that stands for the initial consonant sound of each word.

Topic: Handwriting

Type: Single Skill

Objective: To improve letter formation and spelling

Material: Handwriting samples to copy
Paper and pencil

Display:

Student Directions:
1. Pick a paper.
2. Write what's on the paper.
3. Do six different papers to finish the Center.

Evaluation:
Compare your writing with sample.
Check letter formation chart.

Topic: Motor Skills

Type: Skill (multi-reading)

Objective: To practice visual and motor skills.

Materials: Box station with shapes to trace, templates to trace, papers, pencils, scissors, paste

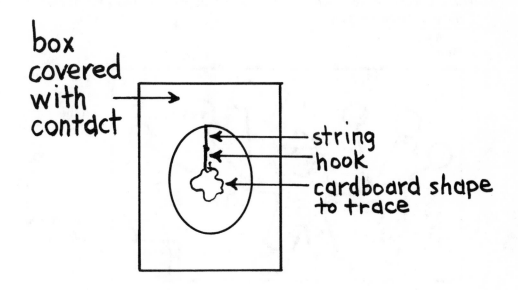

box
covered
with
contact

string
hook
cardboard shape
to trace

animal templates
to trace

Student Directions:
    Pick a shape.
    Trace on paper.
    Cut it out.
    Paste it on another paper.   (Opt.)

Evaluation:
    Place your cut shape on the pattern. Does it match?

Topic: Colors

Type: Single Skill

Objective: To have child recognize the colors red, blue, yellow, green, brown, black, orange, pink, purple, and white (recognize the color word in written form).

Materials: bulletin board, crayons, ditto, pencil, paper, covered shoe box with colored elephants on it.

Plan:

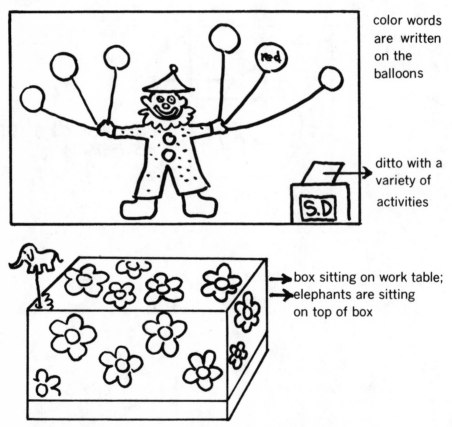

color words are written on the balloons

ditto with a variety of activities

box sitting on work table; elephants are sitting on top of box

Student Directions:
1. Pick a paper.
2. Read it.
3. Draw a picture of what the sentence tells.

Topic: Picture Dictionary

Type: Skill (multi-reading)

Objective: To appreciate how a dictionary helps us.
　　　To learn alphabetical order.

　　Material: Bulletin board display and shelf paper, pencil, picture diction-
　　aries, tape recorder—taped alphabet song

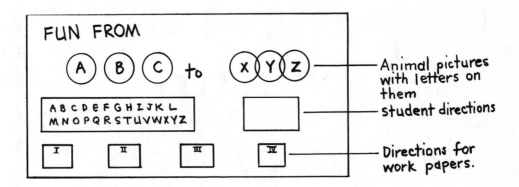

Student Directions:
　　　Study alphabet letters—say them in order.
　　　Listen to the alphabet song.
　　　Do a work sheet.

Worksheets:

I. Find these words in
　　dictionary:
　　Draw a picture for each.

apple	lion
ball	pig
dog	turtle
hen	truck
whistle	turkey

II. Find and list.

　　6　s　words
　　3　t　words
　　4　d　words

III. Find and draw:

　　4 red things
　　8 blue things
　　5 purple things

IV. Find—List*—Draw
　　animals

Topic: Ending Sounds

Type: Single Skill

Objective: To identify ending sounds

Materials: pictures, bulletin board, magazines

Plan:

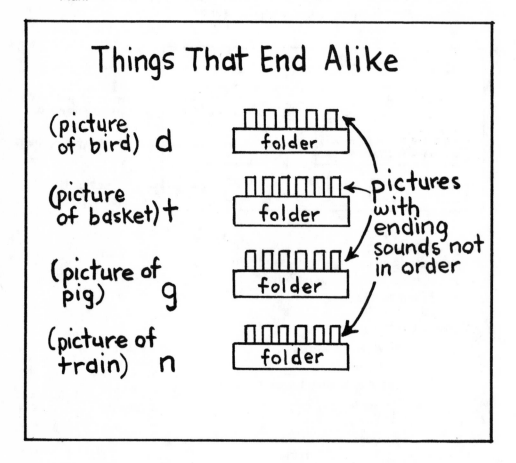

Directions:
1. Look at the picture.
2. Say each picture.
3. Put the pictures in the spaces with the same sound.
4. Show your work to your teacher.

Evaluation: Pupil-teacher conference.

Topic: Classification

Type: Single Skill

Objective: To identify categories and find pictures to match them.

Plan:

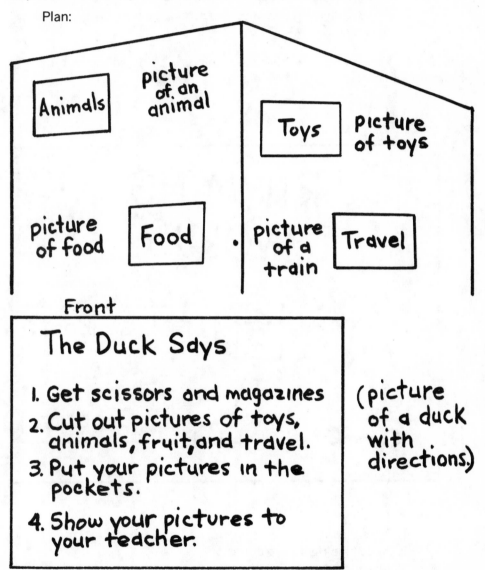

picture of an animal

Animals

Toys

picture of toys

picture of food

Food

picture of a train

Travel

Front

The Duck Says

1. Get scissors and magazines
2. Cut out pictures of toys, animals, fruit, and travel.
3. Put your pictures in the pockets.
4. Show your pictures to your teacher.

(picture of a duck with directions.)

Evaluation: Pupil-teacher conference

Topic: Rhyming Words

Type: Multi-skill

Objective: 1. To have children visually discriminate rhyming pictures.
2. To have children discriminate rhyming pictures and words by hearing.

Materials: Display board, bowls, rhyming picture cards with name of picture printed on back of card, pencil, paper, crayons.

Plan:

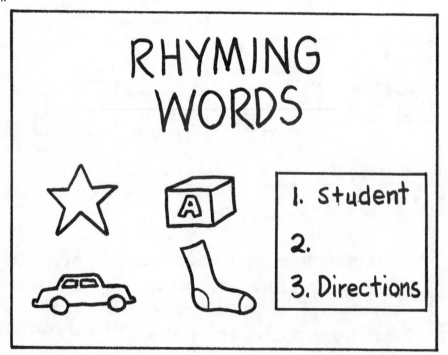

Student Directions:
1. Take a bowl.
2. Match the rhyming pictures.
3. Make the rhyming pictures on your paper.
4. Write the name of the pictures by the picture.

Evaluation: Go over the paper with each child. Can he hear the rhymes?

Topic: Picture Interpretation

Type of Center: Multi-Skill Learning Center

Objective: To increase the children's ability to interpret pictures and then to extrapolate on the situations shown in the pictures through art and creative writing.

Materials:
Paper: newsprint and writing paper
Pencils
Crayons

Display:

How did................?
1. Draw a picture.
2. Write a sentence for the picture.

Picture

What will happen to......?
3. Draw a picture.
4. Write a sentence for the picture.

Student Directions:
Shown on display area above.

Evaluation:
Teacher/student conference in which student interprets and extrapolates through his art work and writing.

Topic: Word Recognition

Type: Single Skill

Objective: To build child's vocabulary.

Materials: Pictures, word cards

Display area:

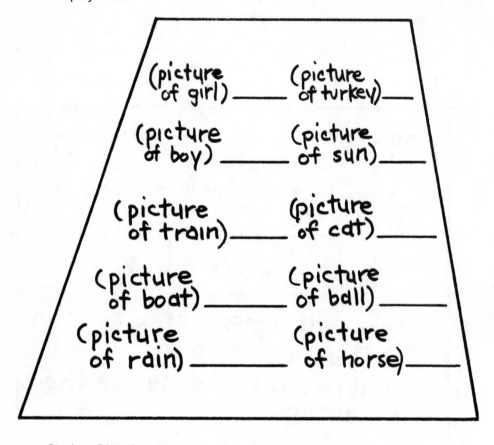

Student Directions:
1. Look at the words and pictures.
2. Take the word cards out. Mix them up.
3. Place the word cards with the right picture.

Evaluation:
Take the word cards from the Center. Use the cards at the Center as a test on word recognition.

FORMAT

1. Title .... Can You Match Colors?
2. Type .... Skill .... Matching colors and color words.
3. Objectives .... Color Identification (Color Recognition)
4. Materials
    a. Bulletin Board
    b. Tagboard
    c. Picture of donkey
    d. Yarns of different colors for tail
    e. Construction paper for colors
    f. Clips to put colors and yarn in
    g. Pockets for colors and color words
5. Display Center

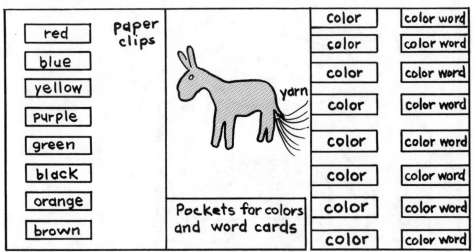

6. Directions
    a. Match yarn with colored paper and color words.
    b. Match construction paper colors with colors in pockets and also the color words with correct colors.
    c. Do papers to go with Center. Do easy paper, then do the harder one if you can.
7. Evaluation
    Some children need much more work on recognizing colors.
8. Key Check Sheet
    a. ✔ Satisfactorily Completed
    b. ✔ Unsatisfactorily Completed

Topic: Root Words

Type: Single Skill

Objective: Identify root words in whole words

Materials: Colorful drawing of large carrot and a rabbit, wagonload of carrots
having root words written on, mimeographed papers of words having
root words, pencil, answer key.

Display Area:

Student Directions: Read the words having root words on the carrots in
the wagon. Take a paper from the big carrot. Beside each word
write its root word on the line.

When you are finished, check your answers with the answer key.

Evaluation: Each child checks his own answers with the answer key. If
he made several mistakes, he may try again another day and note
it on his progress chart.

CLOSING WORDS

THE CHILD. Each child's needs and interests are personal and unique. He operates as a total organism—active and full of curiosity and wonder. Change, in a word, characterizes him best. He wants freedom and guidance. The Learning Center Method is a suggested pattern of organization that attempts to assist the child through guided learning experiences as he develops.

THE TEACHER. The What, How, and Why of Learning Center techniques have been briefly stated in this book so that the teacher can plan learning experiences with students that are appropriate and meaningful by personalizing the learning process of the individual.

THE BOOK represents ideas for action. It has been designed to get down to cases quickly. It specifies the precise idea and related materials through which orderly guidance can be given to each child. The LEARNING CENTER METHOD of classroom organization has a Structure in the Method which serves to facilitate Openness in the Learning Process.

INVITATION TO LEARNING, THE LEARNING CENTER HANDBOOK OFFERS AN ORGANIZATIONAL PATTERN COMPATIBLE WITH BOTH THE LEARNER'S AND TEACHER'S NEED TO HAVE AN EXPERIENCE AVAILABLE TO THE CHILD THAT IS REAL AND INVOLVES HIM ACTIVELY IN LEARNING.

Index